RESEARCHING EDUCATION

Themes in teaching-and-learning

Harold Silver

First published in Great Britain in 1999 by

The Policy Press
University of Bristol
34 Tyndall's Park Road
Bristol BS8 1PY
UK

Tel   +44 (0)117 954 6800
Fax   +44 (0)117 973 7308
E-mail tpp@bristol.ac.uk
http://www.bristol.ac.uk/Publications/TPP/

Harold Silver is Visiting Professor of Higher Education, University of Plymouth.

ISBN 1 86134 177 6

Cover design by Qube Design Associates, Bristol.
Printed in Great Britain by Hobbs the Printers Ltd, Southampton.

Contents

Prologue

Long-standing debates and uncertainties about educational research turned in the late 1990s into acrimonious declarations. Feverish critiques of the education research community turned political heads. The analysis here is primarily directed not at methodological and school-related issues at the heart of recent critiques, but at a wider conception of teaching and learning and of education than the one that has fuelled the most recent fevers.

In the summer of 1998 I had a commission from the Economic and Social Research Council (ESRC), at an early stage of its preparation for a Teaching and Learning Programme to be launched in 1999, and initially planned on the basis of funding of £10m from the Higher Education Funding Council for England. The remit for the commission was to consider existing research and potential research directions relating to teaching and learning, wherever the literature and any other sources might lead. The report was to be part of the evidence that would be considered by a steering committee, established in October 1998 with Professor Sir David Watson in the chair. The territory was immense and in the short space of time available in the summer of 1998 some defining of it was necessary. This meant essentially two things:

- preserving as open a definition as possible regarding the whole of the formal education system and the rapidly expanding features and understandings of 'education' and teaching and learning, including experience in the locations of lifelong learning;
- focusing, in fact, on teaching-and-learning, not on the specifics of teaching *or* learning (styles, cognition, theories of learning ...), large areas of which, given my academic and research background, I was in any case not equipped to evaluate.

There was an element of 'recent history' in all of this that appealed to my interests. Though research on higher education has occupied most of my research effort in the past decade, a project that involved strengthening my sense of the importance of education outside the formal system (working at library shelves I did not normally visit) was an attractive challenge. The openness of the ESRC invitation to conduct the review enabled me to take note of the recent (and not so recent) controversies about research in education, and to address what I considered had been a damaging distortion of the meaning of 'education' in the critical literature. The result was a study based in large part on an investigation of a wide range of research-oriented and other journals of the 1980s-90s, books in selected areas, as well as help from a number of researchers and discussions with practitioners in diverse fields of education and training.

It is not possible to name the many people who were willingly involved in the process, by being interviewed, by taking part in round-table discussions, or by providing written accounts of their own research or of work in a particular field. I would like to single out for acknowledgement, however, the invaluable comments made by Professor Frank Coffield of the University of Newcastle and Director of the ESRC's Learning Society Programme at different stages of the investigation.

ONE

Points of entry

Concern about research in education came prominently to the political foreground with David Hargreaves's 1996 Teacher Training Agency (TTA) lecture on 'Teaching as a research-based profession'. Hargreaves echoed some existing concerns about, for example, the scale of much research and its ability or willingness to build on previous research findings. He went further, however, to attack the prevailing educational research culture as failing to address issues relevant to practitioners, and giving poor value for money for the £50-60m or so spent annually on such research. His argument was for 'evidence-based teaching', based on his view that medical research was more effectively influenced by the needs of practitioners and more accessible to them (Hargreaves, 1996). The last of these points was challenged at the time by Martyn Hammersley as misrepresenting both medical and educational research (Hammersley, 1997). The 'political' dimension of Hargreaves' critique lay above all in its implications for teacher education, and the TTA, the Office for Standards in Education (OFSTED) and government ministers were quick to sustain the attack and seek both evidence and reassurance. Yet another aspect of education had been brought into the political firing line, alongside social work and other professions. The TTA accepted the aim of what was initially termed research-based practice, modified to evidence-based practice. OFSTED and the Department for Education and Employment (DfEE) moved to commission surveys that would bring educational research right into the searchlights.

The outcomes were two reports in 1998, Tooley and Darby's *Educational research: A critique*, and Hillage et al's *Excellence in research on schools*. The latter was explicit at the outset in translating 'educational research' into research on schools. The former assumed that educational research meant research on schools and conducted an analysis of 41 articles in four journals accordingly. The categories into which the content analysis of these 41 articles were divided were, with one higher education exception, school-focused (curriculum, 'school/teacher/child', governance ...), including the preparation of school teachers (Tooley and Darby 1998, pp 21-7). The Hillage approach was to discuss 'educational research', including what it is, the subject matter, research issues and so on, but never deviating, in fact, from the basic hypothesis that research on education means research on schools (Hillage et al, 1998, for example, section 2 'The research agenda').

In recent years there have been other reviews of the state of educational research, concerned with assessing its quality and relevance. However, these have also adopted a rather narrow view of education, defining it in terms of schooling. An ESRC-funded research programme in the early 1990s aimed at "increasing understanding of teaching and learning in the context of the recent educational reforms", and nine of the 10 projects funded by the programme were concerned with schools (though one of the others took account of parents' *views* of assessment). The exception was teaching and learning in the preschool period and its importance for primary school teachers (Hughes, 1996, p xiii; Munn and Schaffer, 1996, pp 109-28). Other reviews, one commissioned by the ESRC (a group chaired by John Gray) and one by the Leverhulme Trust (from David Hargreaves and Michael Beveridge), critically examined educational research with an overwhelming assumption that educational research meant studies of the formal system (see Rudduck and McIntyre, 1998). Other prominent members of the education research community have, during the 1990s, voiced various kinds of concern about the state and directions of its research (for example, Elliott, 1990; Bassey, 1992; McIntyre, 1997). Rudduck has traced some of the variations of confidence in such research from the 1990s in Australia and Europe as well as in the UK (Rudduck and McIntyre, 1998, pp 3-11). At least part of the motivation for the most critical attacks on the research has been in the context of attacks on the educational system as well as on 'ideological' research, and some of the critics have accused the researchers of failing both the practitioners and the policy makers.

It is not surprising that OFSTED and the DfEE should want to know more about the quality of educational research. What is surprising is that OFSTED and Tooley and Darby should interpret 'educational research' as 'schools research' without admitting it. The articles examined within the four chosen journals were selected specifically for such a focus. Hillage et al explained their interest as "primarily in the schools field" and in making recommendations for the pursuit of excellence in "research relating to schools", at the same time as concluding that "education research" covers a wide range of subject matter and "educational issues" yet focusing exclusively, not "primarily", on schools (Hillage et al, 1998, p ix).

The profound methodological weaknesses of both of these reports are not our direct concern here, though it is important to underline the relatively trivial basis of the Tooley and Darby report and the unsustainable conclusions that are placed upon it. Chris Woodhead, Her Majesty's Chief Inspector of Schools, characteristically goes beyond even these conclusions with a statement that much educational research is "an irrelevance and a distraction" (Tooley and Darby, 1998, 'Foreword', p 1). The Hillage report is only marginally less flawed. The team interviewed "40 key 'stakeholders'" (Hillage et al, 1998, p 4), and since these included representatives of research funding bodies, the DfEE, national education agencies and local authorities, the numbers of researchers and practitioners interviewed must have been very limited, and even in these constituencies they were 'key stakeholders'.

Our purpose here is different. It addresses 'teaching-and-learning' within a view of education that is not tightly constrained, as in the case of critiques that have used the vocabulary of a considerable, and expanding, territory to cloak just one segment of it. Schools, school teaching and the preparation and professional development of school teachers do, of course, merit sustained research attention. The important point is that discussions about education have rapidly and increasingly taken a dramatic swing in recent years towards lifelong learning and the learning society; relationships between schools, colleges and universities and the wider society; distance and experiential learning; the educative or learning workplace and work-based learning; community learning – the providers and the participants; continued professional development and so on.

Within all of these and others are teachers and tutors, mentors and facilitators, lecturers and trainers. The educational territory reaches out into GNVQs and NVQs; accreditation and credit accumulation; the few score of students in an accredited religious seminary or the Open University's 160,000 students on degree credit courses and 60,000 working on non-assessed packs. The territory includes the most rigorous programmes and the variety within 'continuing education' or the University of the Third Age. Hundreds of thousands take part in the many kinds of formal and informal continuing and adult education. In the home, the classroom, the laboratory, the trade union, the factory, the nursery, people are learners. The computer, the Internet, communication technology, for example, have added a new dimension to the concept of 'learning', to how and where it takes place. Along each of these dimensions of education there *is* a research literature. However relevant the nature and value of research on within-school processes, and the extent of its impact on practitioners and policy makers at all levels, the ways that they have been explored and that the arguments have been presented have been a false trail. Neither of the two 1998 critiques reflects any awareness of the existence of this wider educational territory, or of the ways in which schools relate to it. Tooley and Darby ignore it. Hillage et al accept uncritically a remit that distorts the vocabulary, a remit emanating paradoxically from a government department otherwise engaged in promoting a comprehensive view of education incorporated in its formal commitment to 'lifelong learning'.

In order to establish as wide a view of the field as possible, for the purpose of the present discussion, 30 journals containing outcomes of educational research were surveyed systematically over approximately a 10-year period (some of them included the UK but had a wider, usually European, remit) and the number could easily have been doubled. The ones studied cover a different version of 'education' from that used by the previous critiques. They cover early and adult education, nurse education, industrial, business and vocational education and training, further and higher education. Other journals studied are thematic, as with curriculum studies or mentoring. All reflect active and often extensive research on education. Other journals were also consulted for individual articles spotlighted from other sources, some in disciplinary fields, and a more systematic study could have been undertaken of the many journals in areas like educational psychology and sociology, science education, special needs and educational policy. Books were included in the survey. Advice was taken from researchers and practitioners in a number of fields (for example, further education, nursing, learning difficulties, voluntary agencies). The intention was to pursue the theme of teaching-and-learning interactions in as wide an educational compass as was possible with limited time and assistance, and in order to suggest how remaking the map of 'education' might be undertaken.

The critiques of research on schools appeared when 'teaching and learning', or 'learning and teaching' as the Dearing report on higher education (NCIHE, 1997) recommended in order to emphasise the primacy of the learner, have come more centre stage. In higher education this has been in order to try to redress the balance tilted unhealthily towards research, though the Higher Education Funding Council has emphasised its support for "research and innovation in learning and teaching" (HEFCE, 1998, p 1). With resources from the higher education funding councils the ESRC launched its Teaching and Learning Research Programme to support research "in any context whether it be formal or informal" and exploring connections "among and between phases, contexts, disciplines, institutions ..." (ESRC, 1999). As this review is intended to illustrate, the literature of the whole territory of education reflects research interests, for example, into industrial training, evidence-based practice in the health-related professions, lifelong learning and preschool reading. The ESRC's Learning Society Programme has involved research into guidance services and credit-based learning systems, skills and adults with learning difficulties, continuing vocational training and informal learning in the workplace, and innovations in teaching and learning in higher education. From *some* standpoints 'education' is already seen as a wide-open territory.

What is attempted here, therefore, is a scrutiny of research (and its absence) across a broad range of published literature, offering a selective picture of what exists, and possible directions and implications. There is no attempt here to discuss in detail the meanings and parameters of 'teaching' or 'learning' or the interpretation of what is meant by 'innovation' or the 'improvement' of both or either. The themes emerge from the experience of practitioners or the perceptions of researchers, and in some cases from research in which the two have collaborated. The intention is to 'support' the themes addressed with examples of research that describes and analyses teaching and learning at various phases and in different locations as well as research that addresses the conceptual and theoretical issues involved. Some important or contingent areas are necessarily omitted or included only briefly. There is, for example, half a century of published research and theorising about learning (cognitive learning, conceptual learning, the conditions of learning, experiential learning, personality and learning, children's learning, adult learning and so on) that are beyond the remit of this study. The psychological and sociological differentiation of learners, their learning styles, motivations and attainments, for example, are themes too vast to address more than summarily. Attention will be directed primarily to the learning encounter directly with teachers or materials or mediated by new technologies, in many of the contexts in which it takes place. The encounter is represented by the hyphens in 'teaching-and-learning'. The review is grounded in what has been taking place and, though there is much to commend it, the very recent vocabulary of 'learning and teaching', which mainly looks to the future, has not been adopted.

Current discussions of policies and principles point towards a need for greater theoretical clarity around many of the emphases involved. In reports on and debates about further and higher education and lifelong learning, for example, a range of underlying principles has emerged.

Some of these include: meeting the needs of individual learners for personal and professional development in order to prepare them for adult life and work; meeting the needs of employers and the economy; encouraging and supporting groups in society who are relatively under-represented in postschool education; meeting the needs of citizenship and a healthy democracy. Such interrelated areas of experience and policy suggest crucial issues in theoretical analyses and empirical research. The following review approaches such principles, policies and attendant theories through a selection of entry points. It focuses on the literature, and where possible it points to lacunae in the research, research that is incomplete or inaccessible, controversial or contradictory findings, and concerns about the dissemination and communication of research findings. The review is concerned with teaching-and-learning of all kinds. There are current developments to which no attention is paid, given lack of sufficient information and research, for example, the potential impact of digital broadcasting, the University for Industry, or the use of Individual Learning Accounts. The focus is on themes and supporting examples that have pointed to significant areas of existing enquiry and potential development. The theme of 'learning for futures' below leaves open the possibility that there are other radical and fruitful research opportunities, linked to visions of the longer trend and changing social and global dynamics, that may not yet have emerged clearly in the research community and the literature.

TWO

'Teaching'

The vocabularies

'Teaching' in its more formal sense is an activity conducted in structured educational settings by 'teachers' or 'lecturers'; in industrial, commercial, school and other settings by 'mentors'; in a variety of occupational and pre-employment settings by 'trainers'. It is conducted by seniors and by peers. In many of these locations the description 'facilitators' has become increasingly common. In these settings 'learning' may result from 'receiving' teaching or from independent activity and may be mediated by materials or technology. Teaching and learning, however, are not coterminous since the latter takes place in all social situations, outstandingly in the home. What we are concerned with here falls within boundaries established by the sustained intention to communicate and in the whole range of settings, and often with the monitoring, assessing and possible certification of learning outcomes.

'Pedagogy', a term familiar in modern literature mainly in the context of schooling from the 1970s, raises particular problems. There are assumptions about schooling that make it possible to analyse pedagogy in terms of the 'situation', including the teacher's responsibilities, power and control, the continuity, stability and parameters of the teaching/learning relationship. The pedagogical situation of the school is recognisable and has been theorised in a variety of ways, but in Britain with attention mainly to issues of power and control in 'traditional' or 'progressive' settings. Bernstein's 'Class and pedagogies' (Bernstein, 1975) and other authors' contributions on teaching, learning and the organisation of knowledge (Young, 1971) influentially addressed concerns about authority and control, children's behaviour and teachers' power, the ownership and transmission of knowledge. The methodology of this and parallel research was sociological, anthropological and ethnographic. Two decades later pedagogy was described as "the last corner of the secret garden" and as a word "rarely used in education in England". Teachers and head teachers were described as being able to talk about "almost anything except teaching itself". The strong British tradition of pedagogical research had been sidelined in the national debate about other priorities, "left untouched" (Millett, 1996a, pp 1-2). The research tradition regarding pedagogy has been largely lost in Britain, and pedagogy has reverted to an earlier image of being concerned with teaching strategy, somewhat divorced from the interactive process described by teaching-and-learning. Teaching-and-learning (an alternative would be learning-in-context) is intended here to take account of the workplace, the community, distance and technology as well as the teacher and the classroom.

The effective schools and school development research, for example, has included the teaching and management features of schools, but has not seriously addressed the nature of teaching-and-learning as complex within-school and outwith-school interactions. One leading effective schools proponent begins an appeal for a science or an applied science of teaching with the uncontroversial statement that "teaching is the core technology of what teachers do". Reform, he then argues, has always failed in Britain because pulling the 'lever' of the school has meant missing the 'lever' of the teacher, and somehow the training of teachers is to blame (Reynolds, 1998, p 9). Defining the teacher solely in terms of the school and teacher education, however, means failing to pull other levers. It is a failure that results from being trapped in old definitions. Sir William Stubbs identifies this issue in terms of higher education, suggesting that what he sees there "seems to be about the quality of the presentation via the teacher to the student.... What I don't see is much research going into the changes in the learning methods required when the control over the process moves from the teacher to the learner" (Stubbs, 1998, p 4). The metaphor of the 'lever' of the 'teacher' takes no account of the movement towards new forms of control over the process of learning – not only in higher education and not only in schools. The existing effective schools literature, occasional debates about the value of lecturing or the competence of lecturers in higher education, the intended outcomes of vocational education and training, or the effectiveness of computer-assisted learning, have not generated a research literature on the teacher–learner interaction as pointed as that of a previous research generation.

It is important to emphasise that the discussion here is not about the content and shape of the curriculum or how it is influenced. It is concerned primarily with interaction and with the influences of educational situations (increasingly including the operation of communication and information technology) – what Oakeshott in the case of liberal learning, formulated as initiation into 'a conversation' (Fuller, 1989, pp 39-42 and passim).

Research relevance

Research into this transaction has been sporadic at all levels and in all locations of learning. This is one aspect of the constant complaint that research findings do not relate to the needs of teachers, nurses or other professionals, and the reasons why it is not used by the constituencies to which it relates. There are important questions to be asked also about the relevance of existing research directions to significant extensions of teaching-and-learning situations in the recent past. How, for example, has investigation of familiar issues in teaching and learning related to the fact that by 1998 two million NVQs had been awarded, the University of the Third Age had 80,000 members (and was growing at the rate of 1,000 members a month), and skills and other projects were being run, among many other organisations, on courses and online by trades unions and the Trades Union Council? Some of the issues raised by the present review emerge from the realities of teaching-and-learning in traditional settings, but others relate to the considerable broadening of the contexts in which learning opportunities have been developed. The issue of how research penetrates educational processes, and particularly why it fails to do so, applies, though with important differences, to both traditional and new settings.

There is a long, though poorly researched, criticism by school teachers of what they often see as the jargon, theoretical bias, presentation, incomprehensibility, irrelevance or other weaknesses of research that may or may not have been intended to influence practice (Cane and Schroeder, 1970, especially pp 37-45). Among researchers themselves there has been a more recent discussion, to which we shall return, concerning the isolation or amateurishness of education researchers, and therefore the low level of significance of their research (Bassey, cited in McIntyre, 1997, p 130). There has been extensive discussion in the nursing and healthcare journals of the failure of research to relate to professional needs:

> **As the profession continues to expand its body of knowledge, researching and identifying clinically-effective practice, the impact of that knowledge on health care flounders.... Much published research is ignored because the complexity of the**

> **language and the choice of publication is outside the orientation of most practitioners. (Stevens, 1997, pp 7-8)**

This is a typical complaint, often phrased in the language of lack of impact (a research-related discussion that in education dates back before the controversies of the late 1990s). "Very little of the educational research that is done appears to have any noticeable impact on the ordinary teacher and his work", commented one researcher in 1980. It was therefore right for "teachers, policy-makers and the tax paying public, as well as the researchers themselves – to look for ways in which the present situation can be improved" (Becher, 1980, p 64). A well-known American account of the history of the impact of research on teaching pointed to the weakness of the practical implications sections of research reports and the scarcity of impact data (Clifford, 1973, p 35). In 1995 a professor of nursing research cited a 14-year-old account of why research was not translated into practice:

- nurses don't know about research
- nurses don't understand research
- nurses don't believe research findings
- nurses don't know how to apply research findings
- nurses are not allowed to apply research findings.

This, she commented, "unfortunately, still applies today" (McIntosh, 1995, p 83).

Although research, or participation in the research process, may intend "to empower teachers to take action" (Vulliamy and Webb, 1991, p 234), it may fail to do so in this field as in others. The view has been expressed in nursing that research may be undertaken for a variety of wrong reasons and that a concentration on research may undermine the "curiosity, originality of thought and a thirst for knowledge" (Logue, 1996, pp 63-9). A further difficulty encountered is the failure to consider the applicability of research findings across, as well as within, boundaries. This applies, for example, to the processes and contexts of adult learning and those of children, and vice versa, and to research on innovation and change in industry and the situation in higher education or at other levels. Even what the National Commission on Education called "proven advances" (National Commission on Education, 1993, p 106) fail to be diffused, and issues of dissemination and implementation are therefore extensions of the research–practice debate.

'Under-researched'

There is frequent reference in journals covering adult, preschool and other areas of education to 'under-researched' aspects of the processes concerned. Even where considerable research is reported there are important silences, including in schools, where much that is discussed below is poorly researched. Teachers working with children with severe learning difficulties, for example, may sometimes have a higher-than-average access to research findings, but may still feel a lack of research on how teachers teach and on what happens long-term to such children as a result of particular schemes.

Higher education presents a not dissimilar picture. In recent years there have been considerable developmental inputs into higher education, for example, by the DfEE and the Funding Councils, and some of these have involved research or been on the borderline of research and development. Initiatives by the Higher Education Funding Council for England and the ESRC in the late 1990s, and the creation of an Institute for Learning and Teaching, are likely substantially to expand the research picture. It could still be said in 1998, however, that "given the expanding size of the HE sector, the amount of research and development work going on within HE and relating to teaching and learning issues is nevertheless still relatively small" (Murphy, 1998, p 1). The amount of research conducted on the complex teaching-and-learning situations in further education has been derisory, even by comparison with the recent position in higher education. While further and higher education had been researched less than schools, on adult learning by comparison "the quantity and quality of research ... is surprisingly limited" (Topping, 1997, p 106). The Fryer Report on continuing education and lifelong learning, among the major deficiencies it highlighted, included the fact that "many sorts of learning go unrecognised, are unregistered and remain unrecorded". More needed to be known "about learning activities and opportunities throughout life, in all sorts of settings, particularly in respect of those under-represented in lifelong learning.... We need more research and better consolidation and dissemination of research findings" (National Advisory Group for Continuing Education and Lifelong Learning, 1997, pp ii, iv). The difficulties in areas such as further education and lifelong learning, training and mentoring, point at least as much as, and possibly more than, those of schools to the need for research which grapples with the levers of change.

Training

Training to perform roles that include a teaching function is a feature of recent debate in wide areas of professional and social action. In healthcare, for example, the issue of training may include that of clinical supervisors (in-house or with university or other support) (Bishop, 1998). The majority of a sample of clinical supervisors in nursing "did not know about available models of clinical supervision and had 'set about it blindly' and were 'making it up as we go along'" (White et al, 1998, p 188). In medical as in other forms of higher and professional education there is discussion of the lack of training of clinicians who may teach students while working mainly in the National Health Service (Jolly, nd, pp 54-68). The training of teaching staff in higher education, a matter of debate for half a century in Britain, was an important issue for the Dearing Committee on higher education and was a focus of subsequent developments. In these cases relevant research is scarce, though there is a small reservoir of international research on how such staff perceive their roles (for example, Samuelowicz and Bain, 1992), often not as 'teachers' at all but as members of a discipline (Kember, 1997, p 255).

Some of the discussion of industrial training revolves around appropriate strategies – such as syndicate exercises or role play (Buckley and Caple, 1995, p 206) – and some around the definition of the trainer. One version of the latter is a taxonomy based on four types of trainer: the caretaker, the evangelist, the innovator, and the educator (Anderson, 1993, p 31, citing Leduchowicz and Bennett). Anderson suggests that inherent in much research on roles is a "range of spectra: passivity to action; reaction to proaction; dealing with structured tasks to ambiguous tasks; and low-level 'maintenance' to high-level problem solving" (Anderson, 1993, p 33). The difficulty in these situations is that there are immense differences among the trainers and their approach to training, and in the training of the trainers themselves. The range may be from "sitting by Nellie" to "systematically designed training and properly trained one-to-one trainers", and from on-the-job training to the work of consultants and professional trainers (Buckley and Caple, 1995, pp 203, 258-9). What these authors point out is that the skills needed of trainers are often overlooked: "The assumptions are made that those who are full-time trainers are omnicompetent and that ... occasional trainers need only to have technical competence to be able to train others" (Buckley and Caple, 1995, p 201).

Some of the discussion of training in industry attempts to define the characteristics of the 'good' and the 'poor' trainer, and to set the needs of training in the context of institutional cultures and personal development (for example, Baldwin and Williams, 1988, pp 61-2, 68-9). It also addresses questions of trainer–trainee negotiation (Baldwin and Williams, 1988, p 123) and the need throughout vocational preparation in modern conditions of 'learning for uncertainty' (Brown and Evans, 1994, p 8).

Although this discussion is underpinned by a limited amount of research, much of it derives from the experience of trainers and training. It reflects little systematic investigation of the components of the experience – including alternative approaches to training trainers, the relationship between personal and professional development, the requirements of one-to-one and group training and the philosophies of training.

Mentoring

Mentoring has spread rapidly in the last two decades across many educational fields – including school-based teacher training, support for minority school pupils, industrial mentoring in schools, for students and new staff in higher education, in industry and business, and by post-registration nurses for nursing students. In the 1980s and 1990s "mentorship ... has become a prominent feature of many professions" (Stidder and Hayes, 1998, p 58). In some of these fields, notably the mentoring of trainee teachers in school-based programmes or in partnership programmes between schools and higher education, studies have been carried out (for example, McIntyre et al, 1993; Glover et al, 1994; McIntyre and Hagger, 1996). Even in this field, however, it was possible to state in 1998 that there had been "limited published research in the area of partnerships between schools and HEIs and even less on the development of the mentor system" (Stidder and Hayes, 1998, p 58). One common issue in the literature relating to all the fields is that of defining what is meant by mentoring and exploring the roles of mentors. The range of roles occupied by school teacher mentors or nurse mentors is often described in broad and complex terms. In the latter case the English National Board defines the function as to "assist, befriend, guide, advise and counsel", but in practice there is a "lack of understanding" and "no consensus of opinion about the components of mentors' roles" (Atkins and Williams, 1995, pp 1006-7). The perception of personal and professional development as a necessary or avoidable boundary in mentoring nursing students is a source of confusion (Yegdich, 1998). The mentoring of newly appointed teaching staff in higher education can involve a considerable range of advice on teaching roles, from the most practical (ordering, obtaining resources) to more wide-ranging ones (planning research and implementing new ideas, student relations and support for new colleagues) (Fullerton, 1996, p 96).

Given the momentum of growth in mentoring it is important to emphasise the significance of the range of teaching or support activity involved, its features and preparation to conduct it. Selecting a mentor or a mentee (sometimes known as protégé) and the nature of the relationship can have far-reaching and long-term effects. In business and industry mentoring new employees is often seen as relating to the status and career prospects of the mentor, as well as the culture and goals of the organisation itself (Caruso, 1992, especially ch 2). An analysis of the literature on mentoring in business, mainly between 1975 and 1988, identified 24 significant contributions, almost a third seen as having a theoretical rather than an empirical emphasis (Caruso, 1992, ch 5). Mentoring in industry may focus on 'high flyers' or employees in general, and though the relationship may be intensive and complex, formal or informal, the number of firms reporting training for mentors was found to be limited in the early 1990s (Clutterbuck, 1991, ch 2). Four important features of mentoring can be emphasised as having relevance for this review, beyond the focus on mentoring itself.

First, mentor training emerges as a paramount condition of success for both sides of the relationship, and this is widely emphasised in the literature. Also emphasised is the fact that some support is often forthcoming, but existing systematic training is inadequate. A 1989 survey by the Industrial Society found that "relatively few companies with mentoring schemes gave mentors formal training, although more than half offered some form of support ... only 1% of companies that use managers formally for coaching (a key skill for mentors) provided relevant training" (Clutterbuck, 1991, p 10). An analysis of studies of school–higher education partnerships concluded that for the partnership to be valuable to all concerned, including the pupils, what was required was "training not only for mentors but also for the whole staff of schools" (Glover et al, 1994, p 30). Postgraduate training programmes for mentors working in schools, sixth form and further education colleges, and for supporting workplace learning have begun to emerge in universities (including Leeds Metropolitan and Warwick Universities). Most industrial mentors working on schemes in schools seem to receive some training (Golden and Sims, 1997, p 15). Defining priority roles in these different, complex situations is sometimes seen as needing to be accompanied by seriously thought-out and investigated training.

Second, mentoring situations, even within a particular sector, are extremely diverse, generally on a one-to-one basis, but with implications for the whole of the organisation. In business, industry, nursing and schools there are many examples of appeals for the mentoring relationship conducted by individuals to be understood as important to the entire organisation and needing support by colleagues and at all levels. In the case of business Caruso discusses this need in terms of "a dispersed theory of mentoring", given that from "a developing protégé's perspective, the mentoring function may be provided by a combination of individuals and institutions representing a collective source of help" (Caruso, 1992, p 65). This is one example of the need to identify at theoretical and empirical levels the relationships between teaching-and-learning and the institutional cultures in which it takes place. In some cases, for example the school-based mentoring of black and ethnic minority school and teacher education students (Showunmi, 1996; Jones, 1997), something wider than the institution is also involved, suggesting a different version of the "collective source of help" mentioned in relation to business employees.

Third, mentoring is presented in all of these situations as of direct value for the development of mentors themselves. This is apparent in school-based mentoring, where different models of mentoring point to the need for mentors at a late stage in the relationship with students "to establish themselves as co-enquirers with the aim of promoting critical reflection on teaching and learning by the trainee" (Maynard and Furlong, 1993, p 82). The importance of this situation for continuing professional development is clear, and some of the nursing literature extends the discussion to consideration of the role models provided by experienced mentors for students who themselves may become mentors. One suggestion, arising out of the experience of Keele University in a school-based parternship, is that the process of mentoring "has developed teachers' skills in a way which has promoted their understanding of, and interest in, school-based research" (Dann, 1996, p 33).

Fourth, mentoring is likely to grow not only in the example areas chosen here, but in other professions (for example, social work), and as a result of the expansion of access to learning in outreach and community programmes of all kinds. The linking of computer-mediated communication to mentoring of various kinds is likely to become increasingly important, and in the conditions of lifetime learning new mentoring locations and functions are likely to give rise to the same demands for adequate definition, understanding and preparation.

The literature suggests future directions for research into all of these kinds of 'teacher' and into their relationship to the needs of learners. Peer tutoring has a substantial British and American research literature on which to draw (Goodlad and Hirst, 1989; Topping, 1997), but as in many other cases the development of new learning situations and strategies in Britain calls for them to have a more significant place in the research effort.

THREE

Research and dissemination

Evidence-based practice (EBP)

Debate about the relationship between theory and practice or research and practice has been persistent in areas of professional preparation, and has underlain attempts in recent decades to marry theory and experience through new approaches to study – for example, problem-based learning in medicine and health-related fields, 'education for capability' in schools and higher education, and various types of project-based or 'real world' schemes. Our main concern here is with the availability and uses of research and the attitudes of teachers to its potential influence on learning. Attempts to bring research into practice and professional preparation have been most apparent in medicine and healthcare and in teacher education, under the banner of evidence-based practice (EBP). The EBP emphasis in these professions is primarily on using research to produce the evidence available and on encouraging its use in practice, as well as on encouraging practitioner research. The latter also has a lengthy history, including the kind of practitioner–researcher approach pioneered at the University of East Anglia, and Lawrence Stenhouse's argument in favour of "research as the basis for teaching" in 1979 (Stenhouse, 1983).

In the preparation of doctors, healthcare workers and teachers, EBP is a major focus of discussion and development and is relevant to any research development in teaching and learning. In teacher education the principal argument is that developed by Hargreaves along the following lines. There is a need to change the way educational research is carried out because there is no agreed knowledge for teachers, there remains a major theory–practice gap, the research done is non-cumulative, and the small-scale research done is not followed up and is largely not relevant to practitioners. Hargreaves contrasts educational with medical research, in which there is no difference between the researchers and the users, whereas educational researchers write for one another, without practitioners helping to determine the research agenda. Teachers, unlike doctors, do not see the need for an evidence base. Dissemination is not the issue if the research itself is not worthwhile. Hargreaves calls for user communities to be involved in a new researcher–practitioner relationship, a national strategy for educational research, and for 'centres of excellence' with an "infrastructure to support research of the highest quality on a particular theme on a sustained basis" (Hargreaves, 1996, 1998b, p 127).

Hammersley's rejoinder to this reasoning questions its picture of the production and use of medical research but accepts some of the argument. He agrees, for example, that there are too many one-off, short-term and non–cumulative studies. He points, however, to the inconclusive outcomes of earlier attempts at 'scientific' research in the field. Non-relevant knowledge is needed to influence relevant knowledge, which is the ultimate aim. There are teachers' problems that may not be amenable to solution by research, and teaching cannot necessarily be based on research knowledge. He accuses Hargreaves of exaggerating the contribution research can make. He agrees on the need to clarify research goals, to build research on the basis of previous work and to exercise more care in the dissemination process (Hammersley, 1997). Although Hargreaves developed his position further, particularly in defence of EBP in medicine, these basically are the points at issue. A pilot study by an educationist and two doctors, looking at the Hargreaves thesis that teachers make less use of research than do doctors, suggested that "teachers are not, perhaps, so dismissive of the contribution of current education research in comparison to doctors as Hargreaves leads us to expect" (Hannan et al, 1998, p 19).

At the heart of the debate is the interpretation of what is meant by a teaching profession, a debate that is echoed, for instance, in the healthcare field, where there has been greater movement down the EBP road. The literature reflects the gulf between research and practice and in some cases looks forward to a teaching and practice culture based on evidence, a culture that one professor of health service management argues "does not exist at present" (Deighan, 1996, p 332). He emphasises that the professions allied to medicine are aware of the strength of the movement in medicine itself since the 1980s and this has had its drawbacks in "progressing informed evidential decision-making" in healthcare: "Evidence-based *health care* is still, by the medical fraternity, understood as evidence-based *medicine* and is not perceived as a multi-professional approach to the improved delivery of health care" (Deighan, 1996, p 338).

This balance-sheet of strengths and weaknesses of EBP includes as one of the weaknesses a "lack of the tools necessary to evaluate the impact that the use of evidence is having upon clinical and managerial decision-making" (Deighan, 1996, pp 334-5, 338). A professor of nursing research argues, like Hargreaves, that there is a lack of "continuity of research effort. Too often research is undertaken on a short-term basis …and is not followed up". She calls for "an alliance between practitioners and researchers or between practitioners and a research facilitator" (McIntosh, 1995, pp 86, 90). Other analysts have also suggested the need in these professions for 'intermediaries' to aid the process of communication and dissemination of research findings (Stevens, 1997, p 8), 'interpreters' to act as an "avenue for the entrance of new ideas" (French, 1996, p 117). Another approach to making research available in nursing stresses the "explosion in the amount of research being published" and the merit of reviews which synthesise the literature on specific topics (Nelson, 1998). Although there are reservations within nursing education about the fragility of evidence and the overemphasis on research, a firm statement from within a school of nursing suggests that "the pursuit of evidence-based practice (EBP) by the nursing profession is now receiving considerable attention. This approach emphasises the importance of critical appraisal of the research literature and the use of systematic reviews to establish the best evidence. This requires both reliable evidence and the training of practitioners able to access, critique and use it" (Bartlett and Burnip, 1998, p 1).

A 'critical appraisal' of EBP surveys its role in medicine, nursing, mental health, social work and probation, education and management (Reynolds and Trinder, 2000: forthcoming). There is much in this burgeoning field that is uncertain or unproven in implementation. In relation to teaching-and-learning in these areas there is opportunity for useful investigation. Some aspects of possible directions are pursued below, but an important point arises from some of the above discussion. None of the elements in these relationships is sufficient. It is not enough to produce evidence, to present or disseminate it or to encourage its use. There are, in the teaching-and-learning situation, in all areas of professional practice, ambivalence and resistance. A recent vivid example is that provided by the King's Fund investigation into how to communicate new information about effective treatments to doctors. It found in a particular case that it was not enough simply to produce evidence that old routines were "pointless or even hazardous" and to try to persuade doctors to change them. The Fund therefore mounted a 'communications campaign' in Dorset involving "local opinion formers, patients, nurses, Community Health Councils and getting a prominent consultant gynaecologist to visit GPs – a widespread turnaround in prescribing trends has come about". Referrals for the old operation had fallen almost to zero from an average in most health authorities of 285:"the jargon in the trade is that this is evidence-based medicine, and doctors are likely to come across a lot more of it" (O'Kelly, 1998, p 15). The factors involved in the implementation of EBP prove to be more complex than is sometimes implied.

Research and practice

This discussion raises questions about the ways in which research might be expected to influence practice. The discussion has alluded to research that builds on previous research, that is of sufficient scale to produce useful results, or that originates in a research agenda that practitioners help to shape. It has to be remembered, however, that research may build on ideas or experience and may, on a small scale, influence immediate practice or help to build a research culture. As Bassey and others point out in education, however, it may have low wider significance if not carried out collaboratively on carefully chosen issues (cited in McIntyre, 1997, p 130). There are also reservations in nursing on the ultimate value of small-scale, small-sample research (McIntosh, 1995, p 86; Dickson, 1996, p 11). Practitioners may not have the opportunity to reflect on the researchable dimensions of their experience, some of which may not, as Hammersley suggests, be researchable. In spite of these reservations, there are obvious advantages for practitioners engaging in such research, often including into their own practice and its impact on learning, as part of masters' and other postgraduate or continuing professional programmes. In areas of classroom practice, equal opportunities or the impact of educational policies, collaboration between practitioners in schools and higher education researchers does take place. Research may reach or be generated in practice in many ways.

Research does, of course, also arise in a sequence. For example, the Catch Up project at Oxford Brookes University on young children not reaching expected achievement levels in reading grew out of a small project that began with 15 children in two schools. It drew on existing research, had follow-up activities and resulted in the formulation of three teaching methods tested in practice. It drew funding from a number of sources, including World in Need, for a major development, the production of materials, Inset provision and other forms of teacher support, and the possibility of continuing research on the impact of the programme. This process has generated such questions about research as to why it is done, who the audience is, who can be helped and how research can be integrated into practical projects. A number of related evaluation and continuing research activities have therefore developed (Clipson-Boyles, 1998). Criticisms of research projects as self-contained or isolated may often be well founded, but this example is illustrative of the way in which many research efforts gather momentum. The experience of university or national seed corn funding provides many similar examples.

The ways in which research develops and points with varying degrees of clarity and success to practice are complex and fundamental issues, but generalisation across fields, however desirable, is extremely problematic. The history of a discipline or a profession, of the great range of institutions and organisations under consideration here within and beyond the traditional educational system, strongly shapes attitudes towards theory, research and practice. Professionals are comfortable – "at ease and confident" in one comment on nurses with their ingrained sense of the history of nursing (Carter, 1996, p 35) – within established traditions. Reaching into this sense of confidence in order to achieve change is one of the challenges faced by research intended to have direct (and to a large extent also indirect) influence.

Dissemination and implementation

The dissemination of research in forms accessible to and likely to influence practitioners is another persistent issue. Practitioner research has difficulty in finding acceptance for publication in refereed journals, which in turn may rarely be seen by practitioners. Sending out copies of reports "has been proved to be a largely inefficient method of promoting behaviour change" and a centralised approach "to implementing new practice is unlikely to achieve changes in behaviour" (French, 1996, p 115, citing research on dissemination by Freemantle and Watt, and Rogers). Project research findings under many different auspices and for varying reasons may remain in filing cabinets.

The Teacher Training Agency (TTA) has experimented with a three-year programme for the provision of small grants to teachers for the dissemination of MA and PhD work relevant to the improvement of classroom practice. Thirty such grants of £400 were offered in 1996 under this 'Off the Shelf' scheme, after consultation with the British

Education Research Association and others, but for a variety of reasons the response was not encouraging. The scheme was open to some 200 teachers who had completed research projects in the previous two years – only 52 nominations were received, 17 were identified as meeting the scheme criteria and 13 teachers produced summaries of their work for dissemination. The TTA has recognised some of the obstacles to proceeding in this way, and a consultation process in mid-1998 aimed at ways of making more use of this kind of research. For 1999 the sum available to individual teachers was £2,500, and £3,500 for teachers working together in collaboration (TTA, 1998, 1999). One response to this consultation highlights an important reason for the non-dissemination of teacher research:

> **Teachers (and others) undertaking this research clearly see studying for higher degrees in Education as a means of acquiring valuable skills and knowledge which are felt to have an applicability beyond the narrow range of their own research topics. Among these attributes a training in research skills is clearly important (giving insider knowledge about the research process which helps teachers interpret the findings of others and enabling them to embark on further systematic studies which might include evaluating aspects of their own practice), but so are other 'transferable skills' in areas such as planning, data collection, data analysis, critically reviewing literature and writing a report. (University of Plymouth, 1998)**

These insights may be more important to practitioner-researchers than the subject matter of their research, which they may therefore not identify as amenable to dissemination.

Dissemination and the path to implementation for nationally published and available research findings are linked to forms of staff development at all levels of the education system. One school for children with the most severe learning difficulties, discussed for this review, has the research journals on the premises, and invites authors of reports to discuss the work at staff development days or other Inset training. Staff at one further education college that was discussed encounter some research in the staff development process. The induction and other arrangements for staff development in higher education (perhaps accredited by the Staff and Educational Development Association, and planned for new forms of accreditation under the Institute for Learning andTeaching) may incorporate research findings from a variety of sources. The Law Society underlines the importance of continuing staff development for staff teaching law at degree or professional levels in universities and colleges, and this "might contain reference to research and updating appropriate to these levels of teaching" (Law Society and Council of Legal Education, nd, para 5.1). Research findings are regularly made available to students on a range of other professional and updating courses, with what degree of success is an evaluation issue sometimes undertaken only short-term and locally.

It has not been possible here to explore in detail the relevance of these issues of research dissemination and use to other areas. Journals such as *Adults Learning, Mentoring and Tutoring, British Journal of Education and Work, Support for Learning,* and European and International journals such as the *Journal of European Industrial Training* and *European Early Childhood Education Research Journal* carry varying amounts of practitioner-oriented research reporting or original articles. Some journals, notably in industrial training, carry annotated bibliographies designed to assist people managing or engaged in training. Further systematic research on dissemination and related issues in such areas could be important.

The example of access to research in a school dealing with children with the most severe learning difficulties is not typical. Discussion with other teachers, ranging from primary to further education, and in nursing, suggests both difficulty of access to research findings and resistance normally associated with the amount of pressure on practitioners or the inflexible structures within which they work. Further education staff may not have easy access through their college libraries to research on teaching-and-learning, and information about new research will, if found at all, be derived from the *Times Education Supplement* or the union journal. In some parts of the education service staff may have individual subscriptions to journals, or receive them as part of their subscription to national or other organisations. In statutory or voluntary sector social work staff may locate research in journals such as *Community Care,* and in all of the areas with which we are concerned staff wishing to identify research may contact their professional body or increasingly use the Internet. It is the *Times Education Supplement* that seems to crop up most frequently. All of this, of course, raises questions of resistance to the use of research, and these are discussed below.

FOUR

Motivation and learning

Theory

The research-based literature on learning and learners, as we have emphasised, is abundant. It is impossible to survey it briefly, but there are a small number of aspects to which it is helpful to draw attention. The most relevant here is the growing interest in social cognition, particularly from the late 1970s (for example, Rosenthal and Zimmerman, 1978; Forgas, 1981). Learning and cognition offer an enormously wide spectrum of research directions, but there is a point about theory that needs to be made. In the field of lifelong learning, Coffield in 1988 welcomes the government's Green Paper *The Learning Age*, following the Fryer Report on *Learning for the 21st century* (National Advisory Group for Continuing Education and Lifelong Learning, 1997) and its call for "an individual learning revolution". It is worth pursuing Coffield's argument:

> There is ... a significant silence at the heart of both reports ... there is no discussion of any kind of the central concept of learning. In all the plans to put learners first, to invest in learning, to widen participation, to set targets, to develop skills, to open up access, to raise standards, and to develop a national framework of qualifications, there is no mention of a theory (or theories) of learning to drive the whole project. It is as though there existed in the UK such widespread understanding of, and agreement about, the processes of learning and teaching that comment was thought superfluous ... no learning society can be created without an appropriate theory of learning. (Coffield, 1998, p 4)

Coffield suggests that implicit in *The Learning Age* is a traditional 'transmission' model, in which those who know simply transmit knowledge to those who do not. He believes that research in the social sciences in the past decade by some anthropologists, educationists, psychologists and sociologists has challenged such assumptions and invited us "to rethink what it means to learn and have been developing a *social* theory of learning". The aim of such a theory would be "to shift the focus away from cognitive processes within the heads of individuals towards the structures, relationships, and opportunities, towards the information, resources and culture which are all needed to participate in a wide range of social practices" (Coffield, 1998, pp 4-5).

Before turning to some echoes of this emphasis, it is important to indicate that the lack of a theory (or an appropriate theory) is a theme that surfaces elsewhere, arriving at similar conclusions from possibly different starting points. Ranson and colleagues, for example, in 1996 issued a warning that persistent demands for an improvement in the quality of learning in schools failed to take account of "fundamental issues facing education in a period of social transformation", notably the need "*to learn about disadvantage*":

> **What is missing is any sense of how learning must be reconceived in terms of the crushing effect of structural transformations that fragment and radically disrupt human experience. *There is a need to develop a theory of learning that meets the challenge of these transformations....* It is only by changing the sense that students have of themselves as learners that they can begin to develop their capacities and realise their potential. (Ranson et al, 1996, pp 9-11)**

Both of these discussions emphasise the absence of a theory of learning adequate for transformed social realities. In the applications of technology to learning it was also pointed out in 1998 that "there is a shortage of good working models of learning enhanced by technology" (CTI, 1998, p 7), and working models of this kind of learning also require a basis in theories that encompass significant change.

There are other theories of learning that relate to questions of attainment and the measurement of outcomes. Learning and the development of National Vocational Qualifications (NVQs) were linked by Jessup to competence, defined as "the standard required successfully to perform an activity or function". The model links learning objectives or outcomes with performance criteria and assessment, intended to "make learning more attractive". The emphasis is on individual accomplishment of tasks within a framework of continuous and thorough assessment (Jessup, 1991, pp 25, 32, 135-8). The NVQ model and its extension to GNVQs were widely criticised, however, as narrow and unrelated to the real needs of a comprehensive vocational and academic framework (Hodgson and Spours, 1997). What is important here is the wider emphasis that "shifts the focus from a concentration on individual cognitive processes to the social relationships and arrangements which shape, for instance, positive and negative 'learner identities'" – an emphasis which also addresses issues of inequalities and structural barriers (Coffield, 1999, pp 6, 17-20).

These discussions have direct relevance for issues of the motivation of learners. Participation in 'social practices' such as lifelong learning and bringing to learning the effects of 'structural transformations' are frameworks within which motivation has to be considered.

Motivation

This discussion, as we have emphasised, is not directly concerned with learning styles and their relevance to improving learning, with some exceptions referred to below. Modes or hierarchies of learning, for example, are the subject of extensive literatures, in the former case to identify individual learning characteristics and in the latter case to approach, for instance, managerial and organisational learning. The purpose of the analysis here is to identify some of the factors that help to construct attitudes to learning.

When the Carnegie Foundation for the Advancement of Teaching in the United States reported the need for undergraduates to enjoy 'inquiry-based learning' (Cornwell and Marcus, 1998, p 12) it was not presupposing a category of learner. When a British project offered "models for independence in learning" it was concerned with *Developing independence in learning*, the emphasis being on development and not a taxonomy of learners (Lewis and Allan, 1996; Allan et al, 1996). Entwistle, in a 1998 study of "motivating students in higher education" began by contrasting "a conventional psychological view of motivation as a stable individual trait with one which recognizes the role of teaching in motivating students" (Entwistle, 1998, p 15). This is, of course, not only the teacher's role. The National Commission on Education acknowledged how flexible learning strategies can increase motivation for pupils of all ages and abilities: "they worked harder and for longer on more effective learning activities" (National Commission on Education, 1993, pp 87-91). Approaches such as this are held to reinforce motivation in areas such as industrial training and continuing professional development.

One of the factors underlined in some of the research literature as militating against motivation (and attainment) is the stress or fear engendered by entry into particular learning situations. This may be the case with older students entering environments with a large majority of younger students, or the uninitiated entering an environment of technologically more advanced students. Reactions may be mixed. A study of qualified nurses attending modules to become proficient as mentors who teach, support and assess nursing students found acute stress related to their re-entering education. They had previously experienced traditional, didactic teaching and the new course was based on a reflective 'action learning' strategy:

> **Fear was experienced when they were not learning what their teachers expected, and an opposing threat came from their peers if they were perceived as 'doing well'. This feeling of being threatened when learning arose consistently across groups and represented the majority of the students' experiences. For most, learning had become a competitive experience surrounded by fear and humiliation. (Lavelle et al, 1997, p 267)**

Re-entry of this kind into a contrasting learning environment also occurs in further education. The expanding and disparate student population of many, typically inner-city, further education colleges includes students re-entering education after having failed at school and often from disadvantaged backgrounds. They may find difficulty in organising their time in the new situation and coping with the paper work attached to GNVQs for example, and the stress involved helps to explain the drop-out rate.

The question of stress and its management arises in research on children, nurses, teachers, adult learners and others, but the research has limitations. Literature (some of which points to a shortage of research) tends to be around themes such as 'Understanding nursing students' stress' (Sawatzky, 1998) or 'Helping children manage stress' (Robson et al, 1995), but the 'understanding' and 'helping' rarely extend to considering the impact of stress on learning.

It is important that none of the barriers or difficulties experienced at different points in people's lives are without a history, expressed in terms of common patterns of learning development or attitudes, in terms of personal choices, or in a combination of the two. It is this discussion that leads to the concept of 'learner identities'. A Learning Society Programme investigation into patterns of participation in adult education and training addresses the influences on whether individuals choose to participate. This is not just a question of knowledge of opportunities available, but also of how adults come to recognise them and make their choices:

> **In the particular context of educational experience through the life-course, we suggest that a key concept in understanding the latter is that of 'learner identity' ... [which] encapsulates how individuals come to view the process of learning and, accordingly, provides the framework through which alternative courses of educational action are evaluated. (Rees et al, 1997, pp 14-15)**

This combination of personal and social explanations throughout the 'life-course' influences not only the choices under discussion in adult education, but also the continuing experiences of learning, the expectations, the stress, the accomplishment.

Differences

In relation to social, racial and ethnic differences there has, since the 1950s particularly, been a considerable research literature that is primarily concerned with relationships between background and attainment. From relationships between social class and education, the research moved into race and gender, and has more recently focused on age in the context of lifelong learning. Coffield and Ranson argue, as we have seen, for a more penetrating approach to learning theories in the important contexts of social transformations, and the wider discussion of research directions needed can only be touched upon here. There are a number of distinct general points to be made.

First, it has constantly to be borne in mind that there are differences in individual learning styles that face teachers in all situations, research on which has been strongly influenced by Kolb's work in the 1960s-70s on 'learning modes' and their combination to form 'learning dimensions', an analysis that has continually attracted research attention (for example, Willcoxson and Prosser, 1996). An Australian study of school 'climate' emphasised the complexity of the concept, especially since "the sense of climate is different for each participant" (Paolettti, 1990, pp 114-15). Aggregation and generalisation must not disguise the reality of individual differences.

Second, race and ethnicity are key features of this discussion, too extensive to pursue here. There is a case for more comprehensive research drawing together, with regard to teaching-and-learning, aspects of the research on multi-cultural and anti-racist issues, research relating to specific racial and ethnic groups, questions of motivation relating to perceptions of schooling, further and higher education and employment opportunities, and factors governing approaches to study. An important starting point for further work is that done by Gillborn and Gipps (1996), which explores *Recent research on the achievements of ethnic minority pupils*. This analyses research on school experiences and achievements, highlighting generally improving levels of attainment in different areas of the country, including those where there is 'significant poverty'. The gap is shown to be growing, however, between the highest and lowest achieving ethnic groups in many areas, and African Caribbean young people, "especially boys, have not shared equally in the increasing rates of achievement; in some areas their performance has actually worsened". The survey is explicitly presented as a contribution to advancing work in this field (Gillborn and Gipps, 1996, p 78). In the context of lifelong learning such an intention is particularly important.

Third, a useful body of research has begun to appear regarding gender differences in learning, particularly in higher education. As late as 1994 some (though not all) studies were suggesting that there was either "little consistent or valid evidence for differences between men and women" in response to instruments testing learning approaches (Meyer et al, 1994, p 469) or that there was little or no statistically significant difference (Severiens and Ten Dam, 1994, p 498). Men were, however, thought to show more interest in qualifications, while women were more interested in learning for learning's sake (Severiens and Ten Dam, 1994, p 498). Different views have emerged. Greasley tentatively suggests a number of differences:

> **One of the most striking is the high fear of failure which women seem to have ... [which] does not benefit the academic performance of women.... Females, however, do seem to have a particularly positive attitude towards intrinsic motivation ... an indication that in the right environment more effective learning approaches may well be adopted by women. (Greasley, 1998, p 111; see also Rogers et al, 1998)**

A psychologist taking part in a project on student motivation had come to the view that motivation, not ability, was "the crucial determinant of how students approach their studies and of how well they perform". He found motivation differences between males and females, as well as between younger and more mature students, "particularly marked" (Newstead, 1998, pp 189, 199). Another report from this project on student attitudes and approaches to studying at undergraduate entry level reinforced the view that women "favoured a deep approach.... Men favoured a surface approach" (Sharpe et al, nd, p 18).

Fourth, this last study also showed that mature students coming from further education "have a more pronounced deep approach than their peers who have not had this educational experience in the previous year". Mature students favoured "the deep and achieving approaches to study", and it seemed that "secondary education leads to surface approach, although the data collected is not detailed enough to suggest that it is secondary education specifically which causes this effect". Age differences alone could be a prominent factor (Sharpe et al, nd, pp 15–17).

Finally, using the now established but still debated concepts of deep and surface learning, the above project pieces together age, gender and course differences in approaches to studying (Magee et al, 1998). Such analysis is, of course, relevant beyond higher education, and alongside studies, for example, of industrial training, outreach and lifelong learning opportunities and continuing professional development, it suggests an important avenue for the study of motivation. It would need to be brought together with other approaches, including that concerned with social or shared learning.

Shared learning

Shared learning has surfaced in this survey in a variety of forms. Some areas of research, including social cognition, relate to this interest but cannot be pursued here. There is, however, a wide range of experience that can be illustrated, but that could be researched more systematically across age ranges than has been the case hitherto.

In primary schools there has been, in Britain as in the US, a rapid expansion in the use of 'circle time', with roots in group therapy, industrial 'quality circles' and Froebelian 'magic circles', and paralleling other discussion-based teaching methods used in schools and adult education. The use of circles, in which children and teacher share ideas on a theme, is seen as having "a potential contribution to make to moral, spiritual and emotional development, to character education, to developing an ethos of caring, to teaching by example, to fostering democratic values and pro-social behaviour" (Halstead, 1997, pp 1-2). Multi-professional education and the teaching strategies adopted are expressed as a form of 'shared learning' in healthcare education. A description offered in this survey related to what was called 'collaborative learning' in a residential setting for lower achievers in secondary schools, where outdoor activities and group work provided an interdependent opportunity to use the experience of the group for self-exploration. Similarly, training in voluntary organisations was described as providing an opportunity to share experiences in the interactive course situation, in pairs or groups and discovering commonalities in experience. In some part of higher education working in pairs or groups is seen as having importance beyond the project or the seminar task or the acquisition of knowledge. In all of these situations of peer learning the vocabulary of 'shared', 'collective', 'cooperative', 'interactive' or 'interdependent' surfaced frequently. Recent work, discussed below, on learning in the workplace has also highlighted that old vocabularies of 'formal' and 'informal' education conceal important trends in how people learn, from one another as much as, for example, from training programmes. These approaches are part of the wider theme of understanding and using the social situation of learners in order to encourage, strengthen and support motivation to learn.

FIVE

Organisations and change

Organisations as a context for teaching and learning range from schools, colleges and universities to community centres and industrial training centres, the military and the professional organisation. Distance learning, computer and video conferencing and e-mail, and the impact, for example, on dispersed populations, as well as home and work-based access nationally, have extended the concept of learning organisations or communities. There is an enormous research and explanatory literature on organisational and cultural change with various levels of theoretical and empirical analysis. The analysis of structures and of policy options in relation to structures is critically important for an understanding of opportunities and perceptions of them. A body of work across the 1990s, for example, considered in depth the nature and implications of attempts to unify the post-16 curriculum (for example, Finegold et al, 1990; Young et al, 1993; Hodgson and Spours, 1997; Raffe et al, 1999). Such work goes beyond immediate pressures for and against structural reform at this level, and has implications for how people position themselves in these structures and processes, and achieve or fail to achieve.

Research on schools as environments for teaching-and-learning has tended to focus on 'climate' or 'ethos'. Research on features of higher education as organisations, although limited, has focused on leadership and departmental structures. Innovation and the 'learning organisation' has been a focus of research on industry and business. A pioneer work on organisational culture in schools by Nias and colleagues identified the factors (history, individuals, forms and locations of interaction etc) shaping the concept of 'culture' and the frameworks within which a 'culture of collaboration' and teachers' beliefs and practices were influenced. The study was not directly about classroom practice, but such analysis as that of learning from difference and by interaction throws light on the ways in which a teacher may behave similarly or differently in classroom and staff room, and how 'school development' or 'pedagogical development' may enable or stifle individual or collective change in teaching approaches (Nias et al, 1989). Although Nias has also warned elsewhere about the "wilful lack of precision" in the use of the term 'culture' in relation to schools, she concluded that "in the past 50 years, and especially in the last 15, the 'cultural perspective' has offered many powerful insights into schools as organisations and particularly into their reluctance to accommodate innovation and change" (Nias, 1989, p 145; see also Strivens, 1985). The roles of headteachers as 'cultural leaders', factors affecting change, the nature of planning and decision making, the relationship between values and organisation, are all somewhere in the literature, especially that on 'school development' and 'school effectiveness'. No clear understandings have emerged, however, from attempts to establish correlations between aspects of school organisation and culture and teacher behaviours (see Reynolds and Cuttance, 1992; Silver, 1994; see also issues of *School effectiveness and school improvement*). A useful direction is pointed by an American discussion of change management which proposes a model of 'organisational learning' linked to policy and practice in school restructuring and the roles of administrators as change agents (Louis, 1994).

There are strong similarities between some of these studies and those on the subject of organisational culture in industry, much of the research being on large corporations. The analysis often focuses on values, beliefs, assumptions, perceptions, behavioural norms and other features common to all organisations, and it tries – generally with limited success – to establish relationships between these aspects of, say, corporate culture and management and other behaviours (Graves, 1986; Ott, 1989). What is generally missing from such analysis is any serious attempt to situate training, and only rarely mentoring, interactively in these organisational climates. There is a considerable literature of organisational culture, and some of it offers theoretical understandings of corporate characteristics (Van Maanen and Barley, 1985, however, describe their work on sub-cultures as *Cultural organization: Fragments of a theory*). The lack of 'serious' analysis of training in organisational contexts refers to a lack of theoretical positioning of this increasingly important area of corporate activity. An attempt is made by Hargreaves to draw conclusions from a comparison of 'the knowledge-creating school' and patterns of knowledge creation and dissemination in high technology firms. He sees schools as needing to rethink the way they conceptualise knowledge creation in order to have an impact on change at the levels of institutional management (Hargreaves, 1998a). If, as is often suggested, organisational cultures are resistant to change, it could be important for the relationship between conservative structures and the need for radical training and other developments to be more systematically explored.

Organisation, in higher education as elsewhere, in Burton Clark's description "is authority, a way of concentrating and diffusing legitimate power" (Clark, 1984, p 109). The ways in which this concentration and diffusion (particularly with regard to leadership and disciplinary cultures) take shape in different institutional cultures have been an important feature of European and American research on higher education (in the US, for example, Tierney, 1988, and Chaffee and Tierney, 1988; in Britain, for example, Becher and Kogan, 1980 and later edition, and Middlehurst, 1993; in Europe, Van Vught, 1989). The question in higher education as in other fields is how the factors involved in these different shapes of organisational cultures impact on the procedures and processes that govern or influence teaching-and-learning. The institutional structures and processes are themselves, of course, heavily influenced by external policies and pressures, subject to policy-related research of other kinds. Institutional and disciplinary sub-cultures help to influence the shape, for example, of staff development initiatives relating to teaching-and-learning, both within and between institutions. A consultative conference on legal education, for example, was told that staff development for improved teaching was inhibited in some cases by not being subject-specific, and "much more could be done if teaching experience was shared between institutions" (Partington, 1994, p 7). Such contexts for the adoption and change of approaches to teaching-and-learning, not only in higher education, invite research concerned with the relationship between context and practice. Although theories of and strategies for change affect the whole of this survey, they are particularly important at this point given the questions of values and beliefs, cultures and contexts that now cluster in the discussion.

How teaching practices and learning environments and situations change are in part a function of the culture of the organisation, and in part a function of how it responds to active participants. Researchers internationally have explored the patterns of change and resistance to change in school teachers' practices. Fullan, perhaps the best known of these analysts, places staff development at the centre of strategic conditions for change and innovation, and in his support Huberman points to the difficulties of trying to change teachers' professional lives at the same time as securing for them a stable environment (Fullan, 1992, especially pp 92-101; Huberman, in Fullan, 1992, p 7). A Swedish research unit explored how and why adult education teachers change over time (Larsson, 1986). The nature of institutional and other influences on teachers has been explored. Such studies range, in one survey of influences, from unintended outcomes of the national curriculum and the local management of schools and Inset to factors affecting changes in the culture of the school itself (Vulliamy and Webb, 1991, pp 232-4). Responses from 821 teachers in secondary schools in England that had undergone a full OFSTED inspection suggested that "just over one-third of teachers expressed an intention to change their professional practice as a result of inspection". The study explored the areas that teachers intended to change (teaching method being the most likely), whether or not inspectors had been critical or helpful, and men/women differences and length of time in the profession (Brimblecombe et al, 1996).

There is an important literature exploring teachers' beliefs in relation to change or resistance at levels of the system from primary schools to professional education. Strong emphasis is placed on the immersion of professionals of all kinds in their disciplinary or professional knowledge (for example, Tillema, 1995) or a pattern of 'espoused theories', views of learning or beliefs and goals regarding the teaching situation (Nespor, 1987; Johnston, 1988). These are clearly relevant to teaching in all the forms and locations that we have discussed. Similarly, resistance to learning may relate to its environment, curricular and pedagogic structures and processes, and underlying beliefs discussed above, for example with regard to nurses' failure to use research (Carter, 1996). On professional development and other training courses resistance can stem from participants' expectations, but also from the culture of the organisation if it fails to bridge the gap between "stated aims regarding personal and professional development and what happens in practice" (Baldwin and Williams, 1988, pp 62-6). In some professional areas courses may be seen as inappropriate or inaccessible to some categories of people (for example, those with young families). Work-based programmes, in association with an academic institution or increasingly on-line, have become more common.

One Australian study of schools was conducted partly because the researcher had already discovered an incredible "continuity in pedagogical practices" over time:

> **... despite a constant flow of new techniques and new curricula, new ways of understanding learning and new forms of work organisation in schools, there appear to be some aspects of pedagogical relations and pedagogical practice which have altered little during the past century. (Gore, 1997, p 214)**

It should be emphasised that there is also a research-based literature pointing to ways in which changing the context can affect people's willingness to change. A report on a teacher–researcher collaboration in studying the early learning of four-year-olds found that in this situation, as the study progressed, teachers requested that research articles and literature be sent to them, and the teachers discussed issues arising from the collaboration with their colleagues. The teachers attended relevant conferences and seminars, and "were eager to deepen their understanding of the content of their practice ... once the teachers had been made aware of the available resources, they were genuinely interested to extend their knowledge of the theories underpinning their practice" (Mould, 1998, p 31). A project on teaching and learning in higher education outlines a range of reasons why innovators innovate, and how they have in the recent past managed to innovate in spite of disincentives in the context of their work (Hannan et al, 1999; Silver, 1999).

This discussion of context and culture suggests a variety of lines of further enquiry, but it is also important to emphasise one direction that is important in general but particularly relevant in these connections. The evaluation of impact is a difficult area of enquiry, as has been found, for instance, in relation to the overall thrust and local activities of major programmes directed at change in recent decades, such as the Technical and Vocational Education Initiative in schools and Enterprise in Higher Education. Too prompt an evaluation may not address impacts that require a longer term. Too delayed an evaluation may face the huge difficulties of taking account of increasing, complex factors that intervene in the process. Evaluation of the impact of staff development courses and programmes takes place in limited ways, and it is arguable that these and all the processes discussed here need to be the subject of sustained evaluation, an activity that itself needs constant review and revision.

SIX

Outside 'the system'

A majority of the issues raised are concerned with the traditional 'education system' – schools, colleges and universities – though with constant references outwards to teaching and learning, for example, in hospitals, industrial training and lifelong learning. It is important to dwell briefly on the extent of this expanding educational environment, and some of the researchable issues that they may indicate.

One of the priorities identified by Elliott in 1990 for promoting educational research was to reach "beyond the boundaries of formal schooling into a variety of institutions and agencies which have an educational function, eg, various forms of professional and occupation education, museum education, community health education, environmental education, etc" (Elliott, 1990, p 16). Ranson, similarly, emphasises:

> **Preoccupation with the statutory sector has caused neglect of pre-five education, post-16 education and training, and higher and continuing education.... There is a need for research into how people learn in the different contexts of the home, community and work as well as within the formal boundaries of school, college and university. (Ranson, 1998, pp 50, 59)**

Such an emphasis chimes in with policy priorities for access to education in the framework of lifelong learning. The Fryer Report included discussion of opportunities through "the availability of workplace learning centres to the families of staff and to people in the local community", "family learning initiatives", and "local learning centres" (National Advisory Group for Continuing Education and Lifelong Learning, 1997). Proposals for the University for Industry have picked up on such themes. Contributions to debate about the learning society and lifelong learning have come from research and theoretical directions and range into diverse and complex areas (Coffield, 1995, 1997; Ranson et al, 1996; Hargreaves, 1997) and the emphasis is invariably on learning as a community or collective endeavour: "the defining quality" of flourishing communities, "and the key to change, is a society which has learning as its organising principle" (Ranson et al, 1996, pp 11-12). Cremin's monumental history of *American education* was a contribution to teaching historians to see education in configurations of activity and experience that ranged far beyond the classroom into churches and the media, the military and the family, and a great variety of other social agencies (Cremin, 1970, 1982, 1988; an outline is in Cremin, 1976).

In the immediate terms of this research review, as we have already seen, this takes the focus into the workplace and the community. The diversity of access to learning within industry includes, in addition to more traditional vocational courses, the non-vocational opportunities at Rover and the higher level programmes devised by large companies alone or in association with universities (such as British Aerospace, and an innovative degree arrangement between Ford and the University of East London). In small and medium-sized enterprises (SMEs) there are problems which include that of release time when staffing is small and specialised, and suspicion of higher education where firms do not normally employ graduates. Discussion of 'learning organisations' or 'organisational learning' encounters such difficulties in relation to SMEs, and though research has indicated what the difficulties are, the directions in which solutions lie are less clear. These may include mentoring (for managers and owners as well as employees), collaboration ('learning networks') among SMEs on non-competitive issues or continuing research into the potential of different learning-support technologies. The DfEE has supported projects in such areas, but the range of learning opportunities and their obstacles, the varied conditions for learning and effective approaches to teaching, remain open to investigation.

An important area of research in this connection has emerged in the ESRC's Learning Society Programme. One project was concerned with knowledge and skills in employment, including the variety of approaches to 'the facilitation of learning' at the workplace. It looked at 'semi-planned' forms of professional learning but found it important to look also at learning within and outside the working group. Learning from other people is a critical focus of the research, in which people at professional, management, team leader and technician levels were interviewed in engineering, business and healthcare. Its conclusions emphasised:

... the importance of informal learning, but it also shows

how strongly it is situated in the work itself and its social and organisational context.... While some knowledge was firmly embedded in organisational activities, other knowledge *was* located only with a small number of individuals – often only one. (Eraut et al, 1998)

Given the continuum from 'individually situated' to 'organisationally situated' knowledge, any theory of a "learning organisation had to take this variety into account" (Eraut et al, 1998, pp 37–48). A second Learning Society project challenged the conventional approach to skill formation, which tended "to focus on education and formal training as the main components". The research pointed to "the case for conceptualising skill formation as a continuous process through time in which learning at work is central rather than a series of discontinuous, one-off educational or training activities". Organisational changes had made the process of "learning at work more central to the achievement of business objectives". Structural, values and attitude changes were producing greater emphasis, for example, on team work and problem solving. The changes required the development of more adequate theories of learning in the workplace and research that moved away from "current preoccupation with education and training as the main components of the skill formation process" (Ashton, 1998, pp 61-9).

Another pointer to the kinds of research possible in this field was a project plotting the learning experiences of people working in six Midlands organisations. This analyses different sequences and combinations of educational and employment experiences over different lengths of time, the nature of the motivation and commitment to study and the relationship of volunteering to learning in contexts of rewards and requirements (Blaxter, 1997, pp 14-16). An American study of the large-scale reliance on interorganisational collaboration in the biotechnology industry suggested some useful approaches to access to knowledge and 'organisational learning' within and beyond organisational boundaries:

Knowledge creation occurs in the context of a community, one that is fluid and evolving rather than tightly bound or static. The canonical formal organization, with its bureaucratic rigidities, is a poor vehicle for learning. Sources of innovation do not reside exclusively inside firms; instead, they are commonly found in the interstices between firms, universities,

> **research laboratories, suppliers, and customers. (Powell et al, 1996, p 118)**

Here, as in many of the situations we have considered, the emphasis of the study and the range of research and literature on which it draws is on forms of organisational and individual collaboration and interaction replacing structures that in the past have been interpreted within 'rigidities'.

What much of this suggests is the need for wider understanding between individual commitment and social (including institutional and professional) pressures for and against sustained learning. One definition of continuing professional development, for example, considers it to be "the maintenance and enhancement of the knowledge, expertise and competence of professionals throughout their careers according to a plan formulated with regard to the needs of the professional, the employer, the profession and the society" (Madden and Mitchell, 1993, p 15). How this extended pattern of relationships between professionals, planning and the diverse and often competing needs of the constituencies concerned actually operates in sustaining the activity is one considerable research area. What kinds of teaching or knowledge access works best in achieving such goals is another. Given, as we have seen, the difficulties that are signalled in changing professional knowledge (Tillema, 1995) this is a third possible area of exploration. A final one includes the often limited perspectives of employers on the release of staff for professional development activities (Chaston and Mangles, 1991, reporting on a study of continuing professional development (CPD) for accounting technicians).

It is important to developments in professional and higher education that increasing emphasis has been placed on the recognition of the value attached by practitioners in these areas to their profession or discipline as the main context within which they see their identity and development. The Macfarlane Report recommended that "training and support centres should be established for each professionally-related discipline, and links formed with the professional bodies for these fields" (CSUP, 1992, p 43). The Higher Education Funding Council for England in 1998 proposed to develop subject networks, strengthen existing subject-based programmes and establish 'subject centres' to supplement investment in teaching and learning through institutions (HEFCE, 1998, paras 12, 28, 31). At the heart of these and similar strategies in other fields is the fact that "professions constitute cultural contexts within a society" (Bromme and Tillema, 1995, p 265).

These industrial, scientific, professional and higher education examples could be supplemented by other forms of work based or workplace-led learning (Bryan and Assiter, on cognitive skills in work-based learning, 1995; Glendenning and Brunt, on workplace-led learning, 1996). There are other ways of approaching organisational cultures apart from those of the formal education system, within which learning takes place (Argyris and Schon, on organisational learning, 1996; Anderson, on learning and training systems, 1993). Some pointers towards research possibilities in wider areas lie, for example, in the learning experiences that have begun to be mapped for rural areas and dispersed populations, themselves being increasingly targeted for improved access through telematics and various outreach initiatives. An example in the South West is the Rural Area Training and Information Opportunities (RATIO) project, establishing a network of computer- and video-conferencing centres for individuals and small businesses (RATIO Regional Challenge Bid, 1995; RATIO *News*). There is a limited literature on rural outreach (for example, Thorn, 1995, on rural Gloucestershire) and a pioneering research attempt to profile the study and 'participation' activities of the population of a small market town, Boston in Lincolnshire (Jones, 1995). These and other approaches to the educational impact of communities and their institutions (libraries, parish halls) and other agencies often involved (Workers Educational Association, further education colleges, university departments) have in common a diversity of under-researched educational activities, that are increasingly becoming the subject of development policy and planning for lifelong learning, including in the context of the University for Industry. Museum education services and public libraries are cases in point. Libraries, for example, have been evolving different approaches to open learning, including materials and training for support staff, bringing "the traditional educational role of libraries to the fore again" (Osborne, 1996, pp 162-3).

The crucial context of all of this discussion is the emphasis, in educational policy and developments on the ground, on the 'learning society'. Differences in definition do not disguise the reality of an accelerating exploitation for learning of all areas of experience and all available resources. The impetus to capitalise in these ways on opportunities for learning (which we can for our purposes here understand as deliberate learning) does not exclude traditional learning locations. It simply requires their reinterpretation. The experience of school, further education or university becomes part of a distributive process which includes home, work, profession and all the other locations we have suggested. Increasingly the discussion has taken in the village or the city as the learning environment, the home and the factory as the classroom. In higher education particularly the country has become the campus, including with the great expansion of distance education through the Open University and other distance initiatives. The process of 'internationalisation' or 'globalisation' is now making rapid strides. The pattern of learning availability or incentive is not, of course, uniform across social groups, individuals and workplaces. In the last of these, for instance, vocational education and training opportunities are often determined primarily by the size of the organisation, with workers in SMEs denied the wider opportunities often available in larger firms (Hyland and Matlay, 1998).

The nature of the policy directions, developments and weaknesses in practices, and needs for further implementation have given rise to important research efforts in education, though not necessarily with clear implications for teaching and learning. The launching of the ESRC's Learning Society Programme was one recognition of the need for research to help translate policy into more radical educational thinking and practice. It followed a substantial period of review and debate about research on education and a growing focus on teaching and learning in all areas of education. The ESRC's Teaching and Learning Research Programme was a response to this focus, announcing in early 1999 that it would have as its "prime objective ... to improve outcomes for learners at all ages and across a wide range of educational and training contexts including pre-school, primary and secondary school, FE, HE, community, adult, and continuing education and the many forms of professional, industrial and commercial training" (ESRC February 1999 Update, www.esrc.ac.uk).

The Learning Society Programme, following its inception in the recommendations of the ESRC's working party report on 'Frameworks and priorities for research in education' in 1992 (Gray, 1998, pp 19-20, 44) has been essentially one of identifying obstacles to the development of a learning society, and exploring and where appropriate challenging existing assumptions and strategies. This has been the case, for example, in comparing the British and German experience of vocational education and skills development in a number of industries and professions; the experience of developing core skills and the experience of innovating with teaching and learning methods in higher education; perceptions of credit-based learning systems; the pattern of availability of continuing education and training courses; approaches to unifying academic and vocational learning in Scotland, England and Wales; low levels of participation in education and training of school leavers; the experiences of adults with learning difficulties; diversity in the post-16 education and training market; lack of progression between the phases of education. Exploring postschool opportunities and motivation for learning importantly takes in attitudes, competencies and attainments at earlier phases of the educational system. A school, just as a tertiary college or a university, has to be redefined not just as a preliminary or a contributor to a wider or a later process, but as an integral part of it, as a 'learning organisation', which is responsive and forward-looking and enables its members to continue a collective and personal learning trajectory.

SEVEN

Communication and information technology (CIT)

Technological development has been too rapid for a broadly conceived pedagogy of technological communication to have been developed, though its adoption as an adjunct or a substitute for certain types of teaching or learning has been accompanied by strong pedagogical assumptions. In schools and elsewhere the use of computers has been a story of rapidly moving experimentation and policies for funding and dissemination. There are descriptive and 'how-to' literatures but research has been in limited areas or confined to the evaluation of specific implementation situations. There is a 'tactical' literature that explores, for example, the dangers of introducing technology too quickly into teaching and learning processes, and the need for consistent learner support, given that the introduction of technology is a basic challenge to strongly demarcated expectations. In higher education:

> **Many students want lectures and tutorials.... They also want guidance and boundaries.... Lectures make everyone feel that they are doing something worthwhile.... Learning technology must be carefully introduced into this environment of attitudes and motives and it must be well supported. (Porritt, 1997, p 15)**

Two common features of the research into small-scale practice are the ways to overcome innovation shock (presumably decreasing as computers become more common at early stages of education) and the importance of integrating computer-based learning into the curriculum (Soler and Lousberg, 1996). Students of all kinds meeting for the first time not just the computer but the use of e-mail or the Internet for interactive learning and communication with tutors and fellow students, rather than the expected didactic lecture and formal seminar, have a considerable adjustment to make. Some of the literature in these regards is descriptive of single-situation experiences, often the outcome of short-term research on the introduction of new equipment or software or a new strategy. Much of it relates to the early experience of computer assistance learning (CAL). There is also a substantial literature, including in a proliferation of technology-related journals, on the technology itself, variations, comparisons, developments and alternatives.

Since the communication and information technology (CIT) resources available are being constantly developed, what is often available regarding its effective use is an evanescent record of its use in innovative ways. As with earlier technologies, including 'programmed instruction' and various kinds of audio-visual aids, there has often been uncertainty or debate about the purpose of the technology – to help teachers improve what they do, or encourage and enable them to do something different or better. In higher education the technology carries forms of teaching and learning interaction on undergraduate and postgraduate distance education programmes, as well as in campus-based programmes where self-directed and interactive learning takes place through access to information, debate and computer conferencing with tutors and fellow students. A New Zealand example reflects clearly the range of aspirations and judgements about effectiveness that arise in specific learning situations:

> **A hypertext program called StorySpace plays a major role in the course: first as a mechanism to bring together in one place the contributions of the lecturer and those of the students, and second to enhance the students' ability to make conceptual links between various concepts and aspects of the course material, as well as between the course material and their own work…. (Soler and Lousberg, 1996, p 5)**

The use of e-mail for interactive learning purposes may have proved disappointing (Crook, 1997) and there is evidence that Internet-based learning has the potential to replace CAL (Tait, 1997) and that more complex learning environments will replace the computer as a teaching medium. These, it is suggested, will integrate traditional text and reference sources with multiple media such as:

> **… animations, sound and video, text-based and voice-based communication facilities (both synchronous and asynchronous) and various forms of feedback and assessment. Creating these rich learning environments is a grand challenge, not the least part of which is designing systems that students**

can navigate without confusion. (Darby and Liber, 1998, p 14)

In the context of distance education an important claim is that:

... the coming together of telecommunications, television and computing is producing a media environment for distance education that is more than the sum of its component elements.... It denotes the convergence of the learning and cognitive sciences with computing and telecommunications technology. (Daniel, 1996, p 55)

A crucial question already arises from the use of such a media environment for on-campus students also: how far or how soon will this picture of distance education apply to a significant fraction of students' on-campus learning experience? In higher education, not untypically, the boundary between 'classroom' or 'on-campus' and 'distance' or 'on-line' learning is becoming more and more blurred.

There is no substantial body of research into the situations in which and means by which CIT can change the teaching culture, though there are widespread programmes of staff training and development to achieve this. For example, a consortium of five universities (Manchester, North London, Oxford Brookes, Plymouth and Southampton) is conducting from 1998-2001 an 'EFFECTS' project aiming to support the development and evaluation of technology into 70 mainstream teaching modules in the five institutions. The project is intended to support "a shift in Higher Education staff culture, reinforcing the professional aspects of the role of the university teacher" (EFFECTS Project overview, 1998). Previous national efforts in higher education under the auspices of, for instance, the Technology Learning and Teaching Project (TLTP), in Scotland the Learning Technology Dissemination Initiative (LTDI), and the subject-based work of the Computers in Teaching Initiative (CTI), all aimed at widening access to suitable materials and helping to integrate technology into teaching. They have tended to be based on assumptions about teaching and learning rather than on any elaborated pedagogy. In some areas, such as work with children with severe learning difficulties, there has been research interest in relation to both motivation and outcomes.

The message from many areas of application, however, is now surfacing more clearly that there may have been too strong a focus on the technology and policy directions and not enough on the pedagogical implications. There is little consensus among educationists and practitioners about, for instance, the enhancement or deskilling effects of technology-based approaches in different locations and learning processes. It is likely that research will need to address trends for technology-focused practices (as well as new applications of digital broadcasting and other technologies) to be incorporated into more holistic approaches for populations of learners at all levels of the education system and in lifelong learning. Schools and colleges, argues a report on *Technology for learning* from BP and the University of Lincolnshire and Humberside, need to place their strategic thinking about the applications of technology in the context of a vision. This needs to be something "compelling, exciting and attractive to those engaged in learning.... The best starting point is the students" and the learning environment that "will best recognise and build on existing knowledge and capability, responding to their needs as developing, independent learners" (Lewis and Merton, 1996, p 19).

One of the most interesting directions for research in this area is the degree of flexibility of time afforded by, and the amount of use made of, the new technologies. One study of the relationship between web-based technology in particular and the workplace argues that it "may help us to re-focus on the workplace as a powerful source of learning" by promoting "learning dialogues. Work-based learning, arising from the purposes of the workplace, requires the creation of just such a dialogue". Here, as in other uses of technology, access to appropriate "support and feedback at the right time" is of critical importance (Reeve et al, 1998, pp 18-22). The potential, use and impact of CIT reach out into all phases and locations of the learning process, and into all aspects of research in these areas. What has often been unclear, in relation to the technology and to learning environments in general, is the direction in which policy and funding can most effectively support learning and change organisational cultures in order to enhance it.

EIGHT

Skills

Key, core, transferable and various taxonomies of skills have been an area of considerable investigation in the 1990s, by university- and further education-related bodies, individual universities and colleges, employers' organisations and others. The DfEE has been supporting work in this area for a decade. From the Macfarlane Report in 1992 to the Dearing Report in 1997, in the work of all agencies associated with higher education and employment, and in research of many kinds, the accent has been on developing students' skills for employment, for independent learning, for successful management of study and career. The Association of Graduate Recruiters identified a group of 12 skills it considered necessary for graduates in the 21st century, focused around the concept of "the self-reliant graduate" (AGR, 1995). An Employment Skills Overview Group was created by the Committee of Vice-Chancellors and Principals, the Confederation of British Industry and the Council for Industry and Higher Education, to promote a national effort to ensure that those in higher education "are enabled to develop attributes thought useful for success in employment and future life". It concluded that much was happening and a consensus on this issue was developing in most institutions, but there was a wide range of questions still to be answered by all the partners involved. Employers, for example, needed to find ways "of allowing their own work places, process, projects and problems to become the *raw material* for student (and indeed the academics' own) learning" (CVCP et al, 1998, pp 1-6).

Many of these attempts to define workplace skills have, of course, been based on discussions by and with employers, but a range of skills (such as learning to learn) assume prominence if approached from other directions. At school level and in adult learning there has been an emphasis on appropriate skills, clustering them differently for different constituencies and purposes – team skills, personal skills that are important to work, personal and social development. Research has tackled the issue of higher education teachers' acceptance of or resistance to the teaching of skills as well as knowledge, either diffused across the curriculum or contained in self-contained units or modules (Dunne, 1998; Drummond et al, nd). The range of approaches to the learning of key skills has been central in recent years to the scrutiny of BTEC and other vocational courses, to NVQs and to the place of core skills in GNVQs (Hyland and Weller, 1996). The sometimes confusing picture (and alternative vocabularies of skills and competencies in government and other policy documents) at secondary and post-secondary levels is reflected in approaches to skills more widely in relation to employment. Discussion of the concepts and purposes involved is extensive in the literature (Barnett, 1994; Assiter, 1995, particularly chapter by Holmes), and has surfaced in the planning and implementation of new curricula and course approaches.

What has been less addressed is the relationship between these emphases and student learning, and particularly the impact on teaching approaches. In a discussion of changing methods in higher education, including a stress on learning outcomes and transferable skills, Walker emphasised that these could be "merely a set of techniques scattered across a conventional curriculum ... but at their best they are devices which help students to understand and integrate their learning through control of information and evidence" (Walker, 1995, p 9). There is little systematic evidence of how widely skills 'devices' are encountered 'at their best' by learners, and with how much understanding and integration. Nor is there evidence of whether and how teachers have adapted their teaching styles and the nature of their interaction with students in response to sometimes quite extensive change. A consultation paper on legal education recognised the connection between skills development and the approach to learning: "The emphasis on active learning will encourage institutions to produce more challenging courses which develop students' intellectual and personal skills". It was the law student's ability to think through information, make comparisons with other legal systems and explore social, economic, historical and other contexts that was important, not the volume of information absorbed (Lord Chancellor's Advisory Committee on Legal Education and Conduct, 1994, p 24).

One area of skills of particular importance in the context of lifelong learning is that of 'learning to learn'. The Macfarlane Report thought these skills of 'self-regulated learning' of such importance to later continued professional development that "they should not be left to chance. Explicit instruction in effective time-management, learning strategies, and thinking skills should be included in the design of all courses" (CSUP, 1992, p 10). In the 1990s there has been an increasing development of 'study skills' in higher education and other levels of education. Adult returners to full- or part-time college or university education or to continuing professional development courses or Open University or other distance programmes are also faced with the need for such skills, as are many employees undertaking courses provided by employers, trades unions and others. The range of potential research in this area is therefore concerned not with the skills themselves (though there is much controversy still over what is meant and where priority lies), but rather with the variety of ways in which they are addressed, and the preparation of school teachers, industrial mentors and others to manage this changed content and context of learning.

NINE

Learning for futures

Research aimed at the improvement of teaching-and-learning is possible across some of the wide canvas attempted in previous sections, though the shape of the canvas will respond to present and future visions and calculations of change in all that affects teaching-and-learning and their relationships, and in the impacts of technological and other contexts. An underlying, crucial cluster of themes that point into the future is that which concerns the nature of democracy and all that pertains to social inclusion and participation, in the conditions of continuing change. The roles and responsibilities of 'teachers' and resources of all the kinds we have discussed are central. Some of the research we have considered sits within attempts to approach possible futures with vision and practicalities, but much of this territory is open to research along lines that may not yet exist. How *do* teachers prepare themselves beyond immediate needs, for a future only lightly prefigured? Schools and the rest of the educational landscape relate directly and yet nebulously to the principles of democracy and its concomitant principles of equality or equal opportunity or inclusion, all open to interpretation. What can an intention to 'improve' teaching-and-learning mean without consideration being given to such issues as the changing balance of purposes available to the whole education service, as well as what is increasingly, if not clearly, seen as learning organisations, a learning society and lifelong learning? How do all of these respond to the early shaping and the reshaping of people's 'learning identities'? How do providers, teachers and mentors of all kinds, on whom lies a responsibility to be alert to the personal, occupational and social dimensions of the learning they promote, respond to the complexities of such a challenge? How do they interpret their role in the profoundly changing contours of 'community'?

These are not rhetorical questions. Education is *now* deeply involved with democratic principles and moral values. Directions in which public debates about ethical principles, politics and policies, local, national and global issues all point are part of the future in which the roles of teachers will be determined. A Swedish study of the 'circle time' discussed earlier reported that it "is generally thought to contribute to the development of personal identity, to increase self-awareness, to foster democratic values and to train children in the complicated rules of social interaction" (Halstead and Taylor, 1998, p 70). This report points to the limited amount of research internationally seeking to evaluate the effectiveness of circle time, and none in the UK (Halstead and Taylor, 1998; see also, however, Goldthorpe, 1998). There are many other features of education in the family, the community, the workplace and elsewhere that may contribute to the pursuit of these kinds of values, but as yet without an available research basis for making judgements and forecasts.

The discussions above also point towards the difficulty of predicting the roles of teachers in schools and everywhere else in the technological contexts taking shape, and in those aspects of education which suggest greater independence and self-direction in learning. Both of these relate back to the emphasis on 'community' or 'cooperative' learning and possible consequential "far-reaching changes in prevailing instructional methods" (Shachar and Sharan, 1995, p 48). There are indicative developments, such as group and student-led learning in higher education, and other pointers in this direction in other locations of learning. Research does not yet, however, couple such developments for the learner and the interactive nature of learning on the one hand, with the roles of teachers, tutors and support structures on the other hand.

There are also, however, dimensions of teaching-and-learning that involve issues of timing and sequence and the possibilities of manoeuvring among emerging credit-bearing and other frameworks and opportunities. There is a strong connection between learning experiences at any one time or in any one situation, but within each phase or experience lies a teaching/learning concern with transition. The transitions are from preschool to school, from primary to secondary school, from secondary school to college, university or employment, from work experience to courses and professional development, from postschool situations of all kinds to local or distance learning opportunities, to all the areas of lifelong learning that are opening and are intended further to open. The transition may be from failure to other chances. This is a question of preparing to make the transition, a commitment to do so, and opportunity and access. Teaching in this context means everything discussed in this review, plus the guidance that will become increasingly crucial to the existence of these routes and points of transition. Research on teaching-and-learning means research on lifelong learning.

There are other wide areas of education that are currently under debate or open to controversy – such as parenting, parent involvement with schools and parent education, the level of formality or informality appropriate in early education, and the place of citizenship or moral or character education. These and many others are on the threshold of futures that could benefit from research into their likely relationship to teaching-and-learning. What is probably most important in considering futures of this kind, by definition unresearched or under-researched, is the strength of their linkages to the wide and broadly interpreted issues of teaching-and-learning that are already configured.

TEN

Directions

This survey of the research literature has attempted to address some of the priority themes and issues in current and potential research in teaching and learning. Running through them all are three underlying concepts:

- teaching and learning in education conceived beyond the traditional 'education system' and in its widest interpretation;
- change and the understanding and management of change;
- the individual, community and interaction, in the context of lifelong learning opportunities.

Without seeking to repeat any of these emphases, there are some other points that need to be underlined. Each of the themes considered discusses present and potential priorities, but the interconnections are obvious. Areas such as motivation, social and other differences and changes of all kinds are related, however necessary it has been to separate them for the purposes of review. Given the imperatives of a more comprehensive approach to educational policy, a more comprehensive understanding of the directions for research is necessary. It is important to have clearly in view the increasing centrality of what used to be peripheral concerns when addressing teaching-and-learning. This applies to 'continuing education'; industrial and other forms of training and mentoring; workplace, home and community access to learning situations, including by technologically provided means, all of which take place outside traditional frameworks. Research needs to reflect the changing balance and the likelihood that, for example, outreach, distance, work-led, community forms of learning and access to global technology and flexible learning systems will continue to gain momentum. The 'learning society' is about 'initial' education and organisationally managed learning in schools, colleges and universities, but it is also about the whole range of developing forms of access to engagement with learning from preschool to adult processes. It is about experience and its contexts, and the experience as expressed by learners and would-be learners has only very slowly crept into the research arena in recent decades, including in relation to part-time students and students on franchised and continuing education courses (Bourner et al, 1991; Haslegrove, 1994).

Although it has not been identified as a separate 'priority' for research, one feature of research and discussion has emerged as suffusing many of the areas concerned. This concerns the social, cooperative or community nature of cognition and learning, in the various contexts of learning and teaching affected by the methodologies and impacts of technologies. This is of particular importance in a period when 'social inclusion' and increased opportunities and access make the sharing of experience for young children, the University of the Third Age or the University for Industry, courses of training and professional development, or any of the other learning locations of learning, of mounting importance.

The research interests reflected in this review are supported and promoted by different agencies, themselves reflecting different agendas and priority directions. The work that these agencies (foundations or governmental) support is not necessarily research-oriented, but it may focus on social issues, including the interest of education in relation to employment, segments of the educational landscape (for example, special needs, further or higher education), or areas of investigation prompted by policies present or planned. Some of the research involved may be conducted by universities or by research organisations. The argument here is not about any need for 'coordination' in an all-inclusive sense, though some degree of collaboration is undoubtedly important. It may be argued that a variety of independent support bodies for research and development, as in the US, is valuable. Research in this wide territory can, however, usefully draw together and build on the programmes and projects of diverse agencies and organisations.

Some of the areas discussed above are the subject of uncertainty or controversy, and will repay being systematically revisited by research and evaluation. This includes such areas as the relationship between research and practice; access to the use of evidence by healthcare professionals, teachers, social workers and others; dissemination and implementation, and research by practitioners as well as by academic researchers. There are major conceptual and theoretical issues involved, in addition to strategic and organisational ones. What counts as evidence and in what circumstances? What aspects of practice are amenable to research-based solutions? How can complex and often contradictory research findings be mediated to practitioners? In what organisational cultures and structures can practitioners readily change their practices as a result of research-based inputs from any direction?

How research engages with either practice or policy is a topic of long dispute. Hillage, in discussion following publication of his report, commented on "how far the research and policy-making communities had drifted apart in recent years but also the challenge university researchers face in closing the gap" (Hillage, 1998, p 15). It is a laudable intention to close the gap, but it is misleading to suggest that the two communities had 'drifted apart'. They had never seriously been together. There is an enormous literature, British, European, American, international on the difficulties of research–policy coexistence and impact, and offering a wide variety of models of possible improvement in relation to education (Silver, 1990). Ministers have leapt into the fray to indicate that:

Research should provide the evidence base to inform and contribute to the decision-making process, but it has often been conducted almost entirely independently of the policy and political framework. (Clarke, 1998, p 8)

Regardless of what 'should' happen, this is also misleading in suggesting that the blame lies uniquely with research, and in ignoring the extent to which the policy and political framework have normally chosen to operate independently of research evidence, particularly if it may challenge firmly held opinions.

The central assumption in much of the debate and controversy has been one of research as a compliant servant of policy. But which policy – the one that is already in the process of implementation or the one that looks into a postulated future? By the time research addresses the latter, policy makers have already taken swift decisions to produce the former. It is also clear from some of the themes discussed above that research (or 'evidence' as it is confidently called) is only one of the sources of principled action by professionals. One critic describes a research-based profession as "an introverted, unadventurous one. For – if this research were research in the sense usually understood by the academy – it would be a profession obsessed with what-is and what-has-been" (Thomas, 1998, p 157). There is certainly no need to detach research from practice or from policy, and there is a need to ensure that individual researchers, research teams, projects, programmes, go beyond simply attempting to "speak truth to power" (Wildavsky, 1979, p 12) – more often than not what proves to be after the event. Researchers frequently aspire to influence, even to be heard by, policy makers, but the process is at best a difficult one. The policy pull needs to be respected, but not to the extent that it focuses research effort only 'dependently' on the policy and political framework. The importance of policy and practice relating to schools cannot be underestimated, but the researcher, in contemplating even a little of what–might–be or what–is–beginning-to-be, has to be encouraged to see processes which include schools, but which incorporate them securely into new educational horizons. The important point about recent critiques of research on education is that they have not understood or addressed research on education.

Bibliography

Abouserie, R.(1996) 'Stress, coping strategies and job satisfaction in university academic staff', *Educational Psychology*, vol 16, no 1, pp 49-56.

Adams, R.S. and Chen, D. (1981) *The process of educational innovation: An international perspective*, London: Kogan Page.

AGR (Association of Graduate Recruiters) (1995) *Skills for graduates in the 21st century*, Cambridge: AGR.

Allan, B., Cook, M. and Lewis, R. (1996) *Developing independence in learning*, Hull: University of Humberside and Centre for Learning.

Anderson, A.H. (1993) *Successful training practice: A manager's guide to personnel development*, Oxford: Blackwell.

Anderson, D. (1997) 'Museums must recognise the needs of all users', *Adults Learning*, vol 8, no 7, pp 178-9.

Appalasamy, D. (1995) 'Mentoring with senior students in a medical faculty', *Mentoring and Tutoring*, vol 3, no 1, pp 19-22.

Argyris, C. and Schon, D.A. (1996) *Organizational learning II: Theory, method, and practice*, Reading, MA: Addison-Wesley.

Ashton, D. (1998) 'Skill formation: redirecting the research agenda', in F. Coffield (ed) *Learning at work*, Bristol: The Policy Press.

Assiter, A. (ed) (1995) *Transferable skills in higher education*, London: Kogan Page.

Atkins, S. and Williams, A. (1995) 'Registered nurses' experiences of mentoring undergraduate nursing students', *Journal of Advanced Nursing*, vol 21, pp 1006-15.

Baldwin, J. and Williams, H. (1988) *Active learning: A trainer's guide*, Oxford: Blackwell.

Barnett, R. (1994) *The limits of competence: Knowledge, higher education and society*, Buckingham: Open University Press.

Bartlett, H. and Burnip, S. (eds) (1998) *Continuing care of older people: A bibliography of nursing research 1980-1998*, Oxford: Oxford Centre for Health Care Research and Development.

Bartlett, H., Wescott, L., Hind, P. and Taylor, H. (1998) *An evaluation of pre-registration nursing education: A literature review and comparative study of graduate outcomes*, Oxford: Oxford Centre for Health Care Research and Development.

Bassey, M. (1992) 'Creating education through research', *British Educational Research Journal*, vol 18, no 1, pp 3-16.

Becher, R.A. (1980) 'Research into practice', in W.B. Dockrell and D. Hamilton (eds) *Rethinking educational research*, London: Hodder and Stoughton.

Becher, T. (1989) 'A meta-theoretical approach to education theory', *Cambridge Journal of Education*, vol 19, no 1, pp 13-20.

Becher, T. and Kogan, M. (1980) *Process and structure in higher education*, London: Heinemann.

Bernstein, B. (1975) *Class, codes and control, vol 3, Towards a theory of educational transmissions*, London: Routledge and Kegan Paul (reprinting 'Class and pedagogies: visible and invisible', 1973).

Bishop, V. (1998) 'Clinical supervision: what is going on? Results of a Questionnaire', *NTresearch*, vol 3, no 2, pp 141-50.

Blaxter, L. (1997) 'Continuity and change', *Adults Learning*, vol 9, no 2, pp 14-16.

Bourner, T., Reynolds, A., Hamed, H. and Barnett, R. (1991) *Part-time students and their experience of higher education*, Buckingham: Open University Press.

Brimblecombe, N., Shaw, M. and Ormston, M. (1996) 'Teachers' intention to change practice as a result of OFSTED school inspections', *Educational Management and Administration*, vol 24, no 4, pp 339-54.

Bromme, R. and Tillema, A. (1995) 'Fusing experience and theory: the structure of professional knowledge', *Learning and Instruction*, vol 5, pp 261-7.

Brown, A. and Evans, K. (1994) 'Changing the training culture: lessons from Anglo-German comparisons of vocational education and training', *British Journal of Education and Work*, vol 7, no 2, pp 5-15.

Brown, S., Armstrong, S. and Thompson, G. (1998) *Motivating students*, London: Kogan Page.

Bryan, C. and Assiter, A. (1995) *Cognitive skills in work-based learning*, London: University of North London Press.

Buckley, R. and Caple, J. (1995) *The theory and practice of training*, 3rd edn, London: Kogan Page.

Cane, B. and Schroeder, C. (1970) *The teacher and research*, Slough: National Foundation for Educational Research.

Carter, D. (1996) 'Barriers to the implementation of research findings in practice', *Nurse Researcher*, vol 3, no 2, pp 30-40.

Caruso, R.E. (1992) *Mentoring and the business environment: Asset or liability?*, Aldershot: Dartmouth.

Chaffee, E.E. and Tierney, W.G. (1988) *Collegiate culture and leadership strategies*, New York, NY: American Council on Education.

Chaston, I. and Mangles, T. (1991) 'Continuing professional development needs of accounting technicians in the UK', *Journal of European Industrial Training*, vol 15, no 9, pp 29-31.

Clark, B.R. (1984) 'The organizational conception', in B.R. Clark (ed) *Perspectives on higher education: Eight disciplinary and comparative views*, Berkeley, CA: University of California Press.

Clark, B.R. (1987) *The academic life: Small worlds, different worlds*, Princeton, NJ: Carnegie Foundation for the Advancement of Teaching.

Clarke, C. (1998) 'Resurrecting educational research to raise standards', *Research Intelligence* (British Educational Research Association), no 66, pp 8-9 (reproduced from *ESRC Newsletter*).

Clifford, G.J. (1973) 'A history of the impact of research on teaching', in R.M. Travers (ed) *Second handbook of research on teaching*, Chicago, IL: Rand McNally.

Clipson-Boyles, S. (1998, typescript) 'The Catch Up Project: raising literacy standards through practical research', Paper presented at the British Educational Research Association Conference.

Clutterbuck, D. (1991) *Everyone needs a mentor*, 2nd edn, London: Institute of Personnel Management.

Coffield, F. (ed) (1995) *Higher education in a learning society*, Durham: University of Durham.

Coffield, F. (ed) (1997) *A national strategy for lifelong learning*, Newcastle upon Tyne: University of Newcastle.

Coffield, F. (1998) 'A fresh approach to learning for the learning age: the contribution of research', *Higher Education Digest*, no 31, Supplement, pp 4-6.

Coffield, F. (1999) 'Breaking the consensus: lifelong learning as social control', Inaugural lecture, Newcastle upon Tyne: University of Newcastle.

Cornwell, T. and Marcus, J. (1998) 'Undergrads lose out', *Times Higher Educational Supplement*, May 1, p 12.

Cremin, L.A. (1970, 1982, 1988) *American history*, New York, NY: Basic Books, Harper & Row (approach summarised in 1976, *Traditions of American education*, New York, NY: Basic Books).

Crook, C. (1997) 'Designing for informal undergraduate computer mediated communication', *Active Learning*, no 7, pp 47-51.

CSUP (Committee of Scottish University Principals) (1992) *Teaching and learning in an expanding higher education system: Report of a working party* (Macfarlane Report), Edinburgh: CSUP.

CTI (Computers in Teaching Initiative) (1998, typescript) 'Response to the Green Paper on Lifelong Learning', with appendices, Oxford: CTI.

CVCP (Committee of Vice-Chancellors and Principals), Confederation of British Industry and Council for Industry and Higher Education (1998) *Helping students towards success at work: An intent being fulfilled*, London: CIHE.

Daniel, J.S. (1996) *Mega-universities and knowledge media: Technology strategies for higher education*, London: Kogan Page.

Dann, R. (1996) 'Teacher–mentor to teacher-researcher', *Mentoring and Tutoring*, vol 3, no 3, pp 33-7.

Darby, J. and Liber, O. (1998) 'The next connection', *Times Higher Educational Supplement*, 18 September, p 14.

Davies, L. (1990) *Experienced-based learning within the curriculum: A synthesis study*, London: Association for Sandwich Education and Training, and Council for National Academic Awards.

Deighan, M. (1996) 'Defining evidence-based health care: a health-care learning strategy?', *NTresearch*, vol 1, no 5, pp 332-9.

Dickson, R. (1996) 'Dissemination and implementation: the wider picture', *Nurse Researcher*, vol 4, no 1, pp 5-14.

Drummond, I., Nixon, I. and Wiltshire, J. (nd, typescript) 'Personal transferable skills in higher education: the problems of implementing good practice', Outcome of a project at the Universities of Newcastle and Hull.

Dunne, E. (1998) 'Higher education: core skills in a learning society', Paper to a conference of the ESRC Learning Society Programme, January.

Earnshaw, G.J. (1995) 'Mentorship: the students' views', *Nurse Education Today*, no 15, pp 274-9.

EFFECTS (Effective Framework for Embedding CIT using Targeted Support) (1998, typescript) Project overview.

Elliott, J. (1989) 'Educational theory and the professional learning of teachers: an overview', *Cambridge Journal of Education*, vol 19, no 1, pp 81-101.

Elliott, J. (1990) 'Educational research in crisis: performance indicators and the decline in excellence', *British Educational Research Journal*, vol 16, no 1, pp 3-18.

Entwistle, N. (1998) 'Motivation and approaches to learning: motivating and conceptions of teaching', in S. Brown, S. Armstrong and G. Thompson (eds) *Motivating students*, London: Kogan Page.

Eraut, M., Alderton, J., Cole, G. and Semker, P. (1998) 'Learning from other people at work', in F. Coffield (ed) *Learning at work*, Bristol: The Policy Press.

ESRC (Economic and Social Research Council) (1999) Teaching and Learning Research Programme (www.esrc.ac.uk).

Evans, L., Abbot, I., Goodyear, R. and Pritchard, A. (1996) 'Developing the mentoring role: some research recommendations', *Mentoring and Tutoring*, vol 4, no 1, pp 38-46.

Finegold, D., Keep, E., Miliband, D., Raffe, D., Sparks, R. and Young, M. (1990) *A British 'Baccalaureat': Ending the division between education and training*, London: Institute for Public Policy Research.

Finlayson, D.S. (1987) 'School climate: an outdated metaphor?', *Journal of Curriculum Studies*, vol 19, no 2, pp 163-73.

Fletcher, S. (1997) 'From mentor to mentored', *Mentoring and Tutoring*, vol 5, no 1, pp 48-55.

Forgas, J.P. (ed) (1981) *Social cognition: Perspectives on everyday understanding*, London: Academic Press.

Fox, D. (1983) 'Personal theories of teaching', *Studies in Higher Education*, vol 8, no 2, pp 151-63.

French, B. (1996) 'Networking for research dissemination. Collaboration between education and practice', *NTresearch*, vol 1, no 2, pp 113-18.

Fryer, R.H. (see National Advisory Group for Continuing Education and Lifelong Learning, 1997).

Fullan, M.G. (1992) *Successful school improvement: The implementation perspective and beyond*, Buckingham: Open University Press.

Fuller, T. (ed) (1989) *The voice of liberal learning: Michael Oakeshott on education*, New Haven, CT: Yale University Press.

Fullerton, H. (ed) (1996) *Facets of mentoring in higher education 1*, Birmingham: Staff and Educational Development Association.

Fullerton, H. and Maldarez, A. (eds) (forthcoming) *Facets of mentoring in higher education 2*, Birmingham: Staff and Educational Development Association.

Fullerton, H., Sharpe, R. and Phillips, M. (in ibid), 'Mentoring at a distance'.

Gillborn, D. and Gipps, C. (1996) *Recent research on the achievements of ethnic minority pupils*, London: OFSTED.

Glendenning, R. and Brunt, J.M. (1996) 'Workplace-led learning: beyond day release', *Adults Learning*, May, pp 230-2.

Glover, D., Gough, E., Johnson, M., Mardle, D. and Taylor, M. (1994) 'Towards a taxonomy of mentoring', *Mentoring and Tutoring*, vol 2, no 2, pp 25-30.

Golden, S. and Sims, D. (1997) *Review of industrial mentoring in schools*, Slough: National Foundation for Educational Research.

Goldthorpe, M. (1998) *Effective IEPs through circle time*, Cambridge: Learning Development Aids.

Goodlad, S. and Hirst, B. (1989) *Peer tutoring: A guide to learning by teaching*, London: Kogan Page.

Gore, J.M. (1997) 'On the use of empirical research for the development of a theory of pedagogy', *Cambridge Journal of Education*, vol 27, no 2, pp 211-20.

Graves, D. (1986) *Corporate culture – Diagnosis and change*, London: Frances Pinter.

Gray, J. (1998) 'An episode in the development of educational research', in J. Rudduck and D. McIntyre (eds) *Challenges for educational research*, London: Paul Chapman.

Greasley, K. (1998) 'Does gender affect students' approaches to learning?', in S. Brown, S. Armstrong and G. Thompson (eds) *Motivating students*, London: Kogan Page.

Halstead, J.M. (1997) 'Editorial; circle time', *SPES (a magazine for the study of spiritual, moral and cultural values in education)*, no 6, pp 1-3.

Halstead, J.M. and Taylor, M.J. (1998) 'The development of values, attitudes and personal qualities: a review of recent research', Unpublished report, Exmouth: Rolle School of Education, University of Plymouth.

Hammersley, M. (1997) 'Educational research and teaching: a response to David Hargreaves' TTA lecture', *British Educational Research Journal*, vol 23, no 2, pp 141-61.

Hannan, A., English, S. and Silver, H. (1999) 'Why innovate? Some preliminary findings from a research project on "Innovations in teaching and learning in higher education"', *Studies in Higher Education*, vol 24, no 2.

Hannan, A., Enright, H. and Ballard, P. (1998) 'Using research: the results of a pilot study comparing teachers, general practitioners and surgeons', *Times Higher Educational Supplement*, 4 December, p 19 (also on Education-line website).

Hargreaves, D.H. (1996, typescript) 'Teaching as a research-based profession: possibilities and prospects', Teacher Training Agency Annual Lecture, London: TTA.

Hargreaves, D.H. (1997) 'In defence of research for evidence-based teaching: a rejoinder to Martyn Hammersley', *British Educational Research Journal*, vol 23, no 4, pp 405-19.

Hargreaves, D.H. (1998a) 'The knowledge-creating school', Paper to the Annual Meeting of the British Educational Research Association, Belfast.

Hargeaves, D.H. (1998b) 'A new partnership of stakeholders and a national strategy for research in education', in J. Rudduck and D. McIntyre (eds) *Challenges for educational research*, London: Paul Chapman.

Harkin, J. and Turner, G. (1997) 'Patterns of communication styles of teachers in English 16-19 education', *Research in Post-Compulsory Education*, vol 2, no 3, pp 261-80.

Haslegrove, S. (ed) (1994) *The student experience*, Buckingham: Open University Press.

HEFCE (Higher Education Funding Council for England) (1998, typescript) 'Learning and teaching: strategy for funding proposals', Consultation paper 98/40, Bristol: HEFCE.

Hillage, J. (1998) 'Forging better research and policy links', *Times Higher Education Supplement*, 4 September, p 15.

Hillage, J., Pearson, R., Anderson, A. and Tamkin, P. (1998) *Excellence in research on schools*, London: DfEE.

Hodgson, A. and Spours, K. (eds) (1997) *Dearing and beyond: 14-19 qualifications, frameworks and systems*, London: Kogan Page.

Hughes, M. (1996) 'Introduction', in M. Hughes (ed) *Teaching and learning in changing times*, Oxford: Blackwell.

Hyland, T. and Matlay, H. (1998) 'Lifelong learning and the "New Deal" vocationalism: vocational training, qualifications and the small business sector', *British Journal of Educational Studies*, vol 46, no 4, pp 399-414.

Hyland, T. and Weller, P. (1996) 'Monitoring GNVQs: a national survey of provision and implementation', *Educational Research*, vol 38, no 1, pp 37-45.

Jelinek, M. (1979) *Institutionalizing innovation: A study of organizational learning systems*, Westport, CT: Praeger.

Jessup, G. (1991) *Outcomes: NVQs and the emerging model of education and training*, London: Falmer.

Johnston, K. (1988) 'Changing teachers' conceptions of teaching and learning', in J. Calderhead (ed) *Teachers' professional learning*, London: Falmer.

Jolly, B.C. (nd) *Bedside manners: Teaching and learning in the hospital setting*, Maastricht: Universitaire Pers Maastricht.

Jones, C.L. (1997) 'The school-based mentoring of black and ethnic minority student teachers', *Mentoring and Tutoring*, vol 5, no 1, pp 25-37.

Jones, D. (1995) 'Student profiling in a rural area: a study of participation', *Adults Learning*, vol 6, no 8, pp 39-42.

Kember, D. (1997) 'A reconceptualisation of the research into university academics' conceptions of teaching', *Learning and Instruction*, vol 7, no 3, pp 255-75.

King, N. and Anderson, N. (1995) *Innovation and change in organizations*, London: Routledge.

Larsson, S. (1986) 'Learning from experience: teachers' conceptions of changes in their professional practice', *Journal of Curriculum Studies*, vol 19, no 1, pp 35-43.

Lavelle, M., Patterson, P. and Iphofen, R. (1997) 'On reflection', *Adults Learning*, vol 8, no 10, pp 267-8.

Law Society and Council of Legal Education (nd, typescript) 'Good practice guidelines in franchised degree courses in law'.

Lewis, R. and Allan, B. (1996) *The independent learner*, Hull: University of Humberside and Centre for Learning.

Lewis, R. and Merton, B. (1996) *Technology for learning: Where are we going?*, Hull: BP International and the University of Lincolnshire and Humberside.

Little, B. (1994) *Supporting learning in the workplace*, Conference proceedings, London: Quality Support Centre, The Open University.

Little, B. (1995) 'Mentoring in higher education: a synoptic overview', *Mentoring and Tutoring*, vol 3, no 2, pp 19-20.

Logue, R. (1996) 'Is nursing research detrimental to nursing education and practice?', *Nurse Researcher*, vol 4, no 1, pp 63-9.

Lord Chancellor's Advisory Committee on Legal Education and Conduct (1994, typescript) 'Review of legal education', Consultation paper, the initial stage.

Louis, K.S. (1994) 'Beyond "managed change": rethinking how schools improve', *School Effectiveness and School Improvement*, vol 5, no 1, pp 2-24.

McIntosh, J. (1995) 'Barriers to research implementation', *Nurse Researcher*, vol 2, no 4, pp 83-91.

McIntyre, D. (1997) 'The profession of educational research', *British Educational Research Journal*, vol 23, no 2, pp 127-40.

McIntyre, D. and Hagger, H. (eds) (1996) *Mentors in schools: Developing the profession of teaching*, London: David Fulton.

McIntyre, D., Hagger, H. and Wilkin, M. (eds) (1993) *Mentoring: Perspectives on school-based teacher education*, London: Kogan Page.

McNair, S. (1996) 'Towards a strategy for telematics and adult learning – NIACE's current thinking', *Adults Learning*, vol 7, no 8, pp 204-5.

Madden, C. and Mitchell, V. (1993) *Professions, standards and competence*, Bristol: Department for Continuing Education, University of Bristol.

Magee, R., Baldwin, A., Newstead, S. and Fullerton, H. (1998) 'Age, gender and course differences in approaches to studying in first-year undergraduate students', in S. Brown, S. Armstrong and G. Thompson (eds) *Motivating students*, London: Kogan Page.

Maynard, T. and Furlong, J. (1993) 'Learning to teach and models of mentoring', in D. McIntyre, H. Hagger and M. Wilkin (eds) *Mentoring: Perspectives on school-based teacher education*, London: Kogan Page.

Meyer, J.H.F., Dunne, T.T. and Richardson, J.T.E. (1994) 'A gender comparison of contextualised study behaviour in higher education', *Higher Education*, vol 27, pp 469-85.

Middlehurst, R. (1993) *Leading academics*, Buckingham: Open University Press.

Millett, A. (1996a) *Pedagogy – The last corner of the secret garden*, Third Annual Education Lecture, London: King's College.

Millett, A. (1996b, typescript) Chief Executive speech, Corporate Plan 1996/97 launch, London: TTA.

Mould, C. (1998) 'The influence of researcher–teacher collaboration on the effectiveness of the early learning of four year olds in schools in England', *European Early Childhood Education Research Journal*, vol 6, no 1, pp 19-35.

Munn, P. and Schaffer, R. (1996) 'Teaching and learning in the preschool period', in M. Hughes (ed) *Teaching and learning in changing times*, Oxford: Blackwell.

Murphy, R. (1998, typescript) 'Educational change within higher education', Paper for HEQED (DfEE) consultation meeting.

National Advisory Group for Continuing Education and Lifelong Learning (1997) 'Learning for the 21st century' (abridged version), *Times Higher Educational Supplement*, November 2, pp i-iv.

National Commission on Education (1993) *Learning to succeed: A radical look at education today and a strategy for the future*, London: Heinemann.

National Organisation for Adult Learning (1993) *An adult higher education: A vision*, Leicester: NIACE.

NCIHE (National Committee of Inquiry into Higher Education) (1997) *Higher education in the learning society* (Dearing Report), London: NCIHE.

Nelson, E.A. (1998) 'The value of systematic reviews in research', *Professional Nurse*, vol 14, no 1, pp 24-8.

Nespor, J. (1987) 'The role of beliefs in the practice of teaching', *Journal of Curriculum Studies*, vol 19, no 4, pp 317-28.

Newstead, S. (1998) 'Individual differences in student motivation', in S. Brown, S. Armstrong and G. Thompson (eds) *Motivating students*, London: Kogan Page.

Nias, J. (1989) 'Refining the "cultural perspective"', *Cambridge Journal of Education*, vol 19, no 2, pp 143-6.

Nias, J., Southworth, G. and Yeomans, R. (1989) *Staff relationships in the primary school: A study of organizational cultures*, London: Cassell.

O'Kelly, S. (1998) 'Lottery of life and death', *The Guardian G2*, October 1, pp 13-15.

Osborne, E. (1996) 'Open learning in public libraries: creating community learning', *Adults Learning*, vol 7, no 7, pp 162-3.

Ott, J.S. (1989) *The organizational culture perspective*, Pacific Grove, CA: Brooks/Cole.

Paoletti, I. (1990) 'Interpreting classroom climate: a study in a year five and six class', *Qualitative Studies in Education*, vol 3, no 2, pp 113-37.

Partington, M. (1994) 'Maintaining quality in legal education', Keynote address at Lord Chancellor's Advisory Committee on Legal Education and Conduct, Consultative Conference, July.

Porritt, N. (1997) 'Managing to learn with technology', *Active Learning*, December, no 7, pp 17-23.

Powell, W.W., Koput, K.W. and Smith-Doerr, L. (1996) 'Inter-organizational collaboration and the locus of innovation: networks of learning in biotechnology', *Administrative Science Quarterly*, vol 41, no 1, pp 116-45.

Raffe, D., Howieson, C., Spours, K. and Young, M. (1999) 'Issues in a "home international" comparison of policy strategies: the experience of the Unified Learning Project', in F. Coffield (ed) *Why's the beer always stronger up north?: Studies of lifelong learning in Europe*, Bristol: The Policy Press.

Ranson, S. (1996) 'The future of education research: learning at the centre', *British Educational Research Journal*, vol 22, no 5, pp 523-35.

Ranson, S. (1998) 'The future of education research: learning at the centre', in J. Rudduck and D. McIntyre (eds) *Challenges for educational research*, London: Paul Chapman (revised version of the above).

Ranson, S., Martin, J., Nixon, J. and McKeown, P. (1996) 'Towards a theory of learning', *British Journal of Educational Studies*, vol 44, no 1, pp 9-26.

Rees, G., Fevre, R., Furlong, J. and Gorard, S. (1997) *Notes towards a social theory of lifetime learning history, place and the learning society*, ESRC Learning Society project, 'Patterns of participation in adult education and training', Working Paper No 6, Cardiff: University of Wales, Cardiff.

Reeve, F., Gallacher, J. and Mayes, T. (1998) 'Can new technology remove barriers to work-based learning?', *Open Learning*, vol 13, no 3, pp 18-26.

Reynolds, D. (1998) 'The need for a science of teaching', *Times Higher Educational Supplement*, 31 July, p 9.

Reynolds, D. and Cuttance, P. (eds) (1992) *School effectiveness: Research, policy and practice*, London: Cassell.

Reynolds, S. and Trinder, L. (2000: forthcoming) *Evidence-based practice: A critical appraisal*, Oxford: Blackwell Science.

Richardson, J.T.E. (1994) 'Cultural specificity of approaches to studying in higher education: a literature survey', *Higher Education*, vol 27, no 4, pp 449-68.

Robson, M., Cook, P. and Gilliland, J. (1995) 'Helping children manage stress', *British Educational Research Journal*, vol 21, no 2, pp 165-74.

Rogers, C.G., Galloway, D., Armstrong, D. and Leo, E. (1998) 'Gender differences in motivational style: a comparison of measures and curriculum area', *British Journal of Educational Psychology*, vol 68, pp 189-202.

Rosenthal, T.L. and Zimmerman, B.J. (1978) *Social learning and cognition*, London: Academic Press.

Rudduck, J. (1984) 'Introducing innovation to pupils', in D. Hopkins and M. Wideen (eds) *Alternative perspectives on school improvement*, London: Falmer.

Rudduck, J. (1998) 'Educational research: the prospect of change…', in J. Rudduck and D. McIntyre (eds) *Challenges for educational research*, London: Paul Chapman.

Rudduck, J. and McIntyre, D. (eds) (1998) *Challenges for educational research*, London: Paul Chapman.

Rural Area Training and Information Opportunities (RATIO), The South West Telematics Regional Challenge Bid (1995); *News* passim.

Säljö, R. (1994) 'Qualitative research on learning and instruction in Scandinavia', *Qualitative Studies in Education*, vol 7, no 3, pp 57-67.

Samuelowicz, K. and Bain, J.D. (1992) 'Conceptions of teaching held by academic teachers', *Higher Education*, vol 24, no 1, pp 93-111.

Sawatzky, J.V. (1998) 'Understanding nursing students' stress: a proposed framework', *Nurse Education Today*, no 18, pp 108-15.

Severiens, S.E. and Ten Dam, G.T.M. (1994) 'Gender differences in learning styles: a narrative review and quantitative meta-analysis', *Higher Education*, vol 27, pp 487-501.

Shachar, H. and Sharan, S. (1995) 'Cooperative learning and the organization of secondary schools', *School Effectiveness and School Improvement*, vol 6, no 1, pp 47-66.

Sharpe, R., Baldwin, A., Newstead, S. and Fullerton, H. (nd, typescript), 'Attitudes and approaches to studying in entry level undergraduate students', Plymouth: University of Plymouth.

Showunmi, V. (1996) 'A black perspective on mentoring', *Mentoring and Tutoring*, vol 3, no 3, pp 12-14.

Silver, H. (1990) *Education, change and the policy process*, London: Falmer.

Silver, H. (1994) *Good schools, effective schools: Judgements and their history*, London: Cassell.

Silver, H. (1999) 'Managing to innovate in higher education', *British Journal of Educational Studies*, vol 47, no 2, pp 145-56.

Simpson, V., Curzio, J., Gillespie, A. and McCowan, H. (1997) 'Evidence-based practice: a case study', *NTresearch*, vol 2, no 6, pp 426-32.

Smith, P. and Masterson, A. (1996) 'Promoting the dissemination and implementation of research findings', *Nurse Researcher*, vol 4, no 2, pp 15-29.

Soler, J. and Lousberg, M. (1996) 'Rethinking the teaching of a university course', *Active Learning*, no 5, pp 3-8.

Sosabowski, M.H., Herson, K. and Lloyd, A.W. (1998) 'Enhancing learning and teaching quality: integration of networked learning technologies into undergraduate modules', *Active Learning*, no 8, pp 20-5.

Sparkes, A.C. (1991) 'The culture of teaching, critical reflection and change: possibilities and problems', *Educational Management and Administration*, vol 19, no 1, pp 4-19.

Spouse, J. (1996) 'The effective mentor: a model for student-centred learning in clinical practice', *NTresearch*, vol 1, no 2, pp 120-33.

Stenhouse, L. (1983) 'Research as a basis for teaching', in L. Stenhouse, *Authority, education and emancipation*, London: Heinemann (reprinting his 1979 inaugural lecture).

Stevens, J. (1997) 'Improving integration between research and practice as a means of developing evidence-based health care', *NTresearch*, vol 2, no 1, pp 7-15.

Stidder, G. and Hayes, S. (1998) 'Mentoring – rhetoric and reality', *Mentoring and Tutoring*, vol 5, no 3, pp 57-64.

Strivens, J. (1985) 'School climate: a review of a problematic concept', in D. Reynolds (ed) *Studying school effectiveness*, London: Falmer.

Stubbs, Sir W. (1998, typescript) Keynote lecture at Open University residential weekend.

Tait, B. (1997) 'Constructive Internet based learning', *Active Learning*, no 7, pp 4-8.

Taylor, I. (1996) 'The role of school mentors – some messages from training in other professions', *Mentoring and Tutoring*, vol 3, no 3, pp 43-9.

Thomas, G. (1998) 'The myth of rational research', *British Educational Research Journal*, vol 24, no 2, pp 141-57.

Thorn, L. (1995) 'Using outreach in a rural tertiary college', *Adults Learning*, April, pp 243-5.

Tierney, W.G. (1988) 'Organizational culture in higher education: defining the essentials', *Journal of Higher Education*, vol 59, no 1, pp 2-21.

Tillema, H.H. (1995) 'Changing the professional knowledge and beliefs of teachers: a training study', *Learning and Instruction*, no 5, pp 291-318.

Tooley, J. and Darby, D. (1998) *Educational research: A critique*, Office for Standards in Education.

Topping, K. (1997) 'Peer tutoring for flexible and effective adult learning', in P. Sutherland (ed) *Adult learning: A reader*, London: Kogan Page.

TTA (Teacher Training Agency) (1998, typescript) 'MA and PhD dissemination: Off the Shelf', Discussion paper.

TTA (1999, typescript) 'Teacher research grant scheme: applications for 1999/2000', Circular.

TUC Education (nd) *Skills 1*.

University of Plymouth (1998, typescript) Response to TTA discussion document on MA and PhD dissemination.

University of Plymouth (1998/99) Postgraduate Certificate in Learning and Teaching in Higher Education, programme handbook.

Van Maanen, J. and Barley, S.R. (1985) 'Cultural organization: fragments of a theory', in P.J. Frost, L.F. Moore, M.R. Louis, C.C. Lundberg and J. Martin (eds) *Organizational culture*, Beverly Hills, CA: Sage Publications.

Van Vught, F.A. (1989) 'Creating innovations in higher education', *European Journal of Education*, vol 24, no 3, pp 249-70.

Vulliamy, G. and Webb, R. (1991) 'Teacher research and educational change: an empirical study', *British Educational Research Journal*, vol 17, no 3, pp 219-36.

Walker, L. (1995) 'The British context', in L. Walker (ed) *Institutional change: Towards an ability-based curriculum in higher education*, Conference report, Oxford: Oxford Brookes University.

White, E., Butterworth, T., Bishop, V., Carson, J., Jeacock, J. and Clements, A. (1998) 'Clinical supervision: insider reports of a private world', *Journal of Advanced Nursing*, vol 28, no 1, pp 185-92.

White, M. (1997) 'Magic circles: the benefits of circle time', *SPES (a magazine for the study of spiritual, moral and cultural values in education)*, no 6, pp 4-5.

Wildavsky, A. (1979) *Speaking truth to power: The art and craft of policy analysis*, Boston, MA: Little Brown, Winter.

Willcoxson, L. and Prosser, M. (1996) 'Kolb's learning style inventory (1985): review and further study of validity and reliability', *British Journal of Educational Psychology*, no 66, pp 247-57.

Winders, R. (nd, typescript) 'The use of telematics in education and training', Plymouth: University of Plymouth.

Yegdich, T. (1998) 'How not to do clinical supervision in nursing', *Journal of Advanced Nursing*, vol 28, no 1, pp 193-202.

Young, M. (ed) (1971) *Knowledge and control: New directions for the sociology of education*, West Drayton: Collier Macmillan.

Young, M., Hayton, A., Hodgson, A. and Morris, A. (1993) *Towards connectivity: An interim approach to unifying the post-16 curriculum*, London: Institute of Education, University of London.

Appendix:
Journals of the 1980s-90s scanned
for the purposes of this review

[Issues of other journals cited were consulted only for particular items.
Books consulted are included in the Bibliography.]

Active Learning
Adults Learning
British Educational Research Journal
British Journal of Educational Psychology
British Journal of Educational Studies
British Journal of Education and Work
Cambridge Journal of Education
Educational Management and Administration
Educational Psychology
Educational Research
European Early Childhood Education Research Journal
European Journal of Education
Higher Education
International Journal of Educational Research
Journal of Advanced Nursing
Journal of Curriculum Studies
Journal of European Industrial Training
Journal of Further and Higher Education
Journal of Qualitative Research
Learning and Instruction
Mentoring and Tutoring
NTresearch
Nurse Education Today
Nurse Researcher
Open Learning
Qualitative Studies in Education
Research in Education
School Effectiveness and School Improvement
Studies in Higher Education
Support for Education

Other related titles from The Policy Press include:

Learning at work
Edited by Frank Coffield (1998)
ISBN 1 86134 123 7 £13.99

Why's the beer always stronger up North? Studies of lifelong learning in Europe
Edited by Frank Coffield (1999)
ISBN 1 86134 131 8 £13.99

Speaking truth to power: Research and policy on lifelong learning
Edited by Frank Coffield (1999)
ISBN 1 86134 147 4 £13.99

Informal learning
Edited by Frank Coffield (1999: forthcoming)
ISBN 1 86134 152 0 £13.99

Adult guidance services and The Learning Society: Emerging policies in the European Union
Will Bartlett, Teresa Rees and A.G. Watts (1999: forthcoming)
ISBN 1 86134 153 9 £17.99 tbc (paperback)
ISBN 1 86134 175 X £45.00 (hardback)

Training and education in urban regeneration: A framework for participants
Paul Henderson and Marjorie Mayo (1998)
ISBN 1 86134 124 5 £10.95

Employer involvement in area regeneration
Alan McGregor, Andrea Glass, Kenneth Richmond, Zoe Ferguson and Kevin Higgins (1999)
ISBN 1 86134 161 X £12.95

Voices within and without: Responses to long-term unemployment in Germany, Sweden and Britain
Jochen Clasen, Arthur Gould and Jill Vincent (1998)
ISBN 1 86134 090 7 £16.99 (paperback)
ISBN 1 86134 108 3 £40.00 (hardback)

The jobs gap in Britain's cities: Employment loss and labour market consequences
Ivan Turok and Nicola Edge (1999)
ISBN 1 86134 160 1 £12.95

All the above titles are available from
Biblios Publishers' Distribution Services Ltd
Star Road, Partridge Green, West Sussex RH13 8LD, UK
Telephone +44 (0)1403 710851, Fax +44 (0)1403 711143